Really Useful Guides
....

Romans

15 The Chambers, Vineyard
Abingdon OX14 3FE
brf.org.uk

Bible Reading Fellowship is a charity (233280)
and company limited by guarantee (301324),
registered in England and Wales

ISBN 978 1 80039 821 5
First published 2022
10 9 8 7 6 5 4 3 2 1 0
All rights reserved

Text © Ernest Clark 2020
This edition © Bible Reading Fellowship 2022
Cover image by Rebecca J Hall

The author asserts the moral right to be identified as the author of this work

Acknowledgements
Scripture quotations are taken from The Holy Bible, New International Version (Anglicised edition) copyright © 1979, 1984, 2011 by Biblica. Used by permission of Hodder & Stoughton Publishers, a Hachette UK company. All rights reserved. 'NIV' is a registered trademark of Biblica. UK trademark number 1448790.

Every effort has been made to trace and contact copyright owners for material used in this resource. We apologise for any inadvertent omissions or errors, and would ask those concerned to contact us so that full acknowledgement can be made in the future.

A catalogue record for this book is available from the British Library

Printed and bound by CPI Group (UK) Ltd, Croydon CR0 4YY

Really Useful Guides

Romans

Ernest Clark

Series editor: Derek Tidball

To the saints at St Andrew's Church, St Andrews, brothers, sisters, fellow workers and patrons.

Each Really Useful Guide focuses on a specific biblical book, making it come to life for the reader, enabling them to understand the message and to apply its truth to today's circumstances. Though not a commentary, it gives valuable insight into the book's message. Though not an introduction, it summarises the important aspects of the book to aid reading and application.

This Really Useful Guide to Romans will transform your understanding of the biblical text, and will help you to engage with the message in new ways today, giving confidence in the Bible and increasing faith in God.

Contents

1	**Why read Romans? A personal reflection**	7
2	**Start here**	11
	Paul's brothers and sisters in Rome	12
	The church in Rome	14
	Paul's main concerns	17
	Paul's desire to share a gift with his friends	18
	Romans' message: God's good news about his Son, Jesus Christ our Lord	21
	Disclosing the ancient mystery	21
	A few words about words	28
3	**Guide to the contents**	30
	Two outlines: the path and the steps	30
	Paul greets his friends with God's good news, 1:1–17	35
	The faithful and righteous God condemns sin but sets believers right, 1:18—4:25	41
	The Son and the Spirit enable believers to live right, 5:1—8:39	57
	God has been and will be faithful to Israel, 9:1—11:36	72

	Paul calls believers to holiness and love, 12:1—15:13	80
	Paul plans an apostolic visit to Rome, 15:14–33	93
	Paul blesses his friends, 16:1–27	95
4	**Romans among the other New Testament writings**	**99**
	Writing the next chapters in the same story	99
	Romans and Galatians	101
	Romans and James	103
	Romans and Matthew's gospel	107
	Romans and Hebrews	109
5	**The continuing message of Romans**	**111**
	God's freedom, righteousness and love	111
	The human person and behaviour	113
	Sexual orientation	114
	The Spirit's life and leading	115
	Faith and love	116
	Faith and civil authorities	116
	Faith and creation	117
	Faith and Israel's future	118
	Nurturing diversity within the church	119
	Accepting each other as God accepts us	120
6	**Questions for reflection and discussion**	**122**
Further reading		**128**

1

Why read Romans?
A personal reflection

I first encountered Romans in bits. Memorising verses like 3:23 ('For all have sinned and fall short of the glory of God') and 6:23 ('For the wages of sin is death, but the gift of God is eternal life in Christ Jesus our Lord') laid the foundation stones of my childhood theology: my sin and God's grace.

Over the next 30 years, Romans continued its role as my school master. In my first year of university, tutored by the ancient African theologian Augustine, Romans pushed me to acknowledge the corruption of the whole human person and God's radical freedom. And it expanded my gratitude for God's mercy toward me to a whole new dimension.

Twelve years later, as a postgraduate student, Romans schooled me again. It straightened up and tightened down some of my theological ideas that were coming loose. And, pointing me back to an earlier round of lessons, it showed me again the extraordinary power of the Spirit's gracious action in my life, how he enables me to live faithfully and love truly.

But studying to write this book, I have encountered Romans as a wise friend.

I have tried to honour Paul by letting his letter set its own agenda in its own terms. I've restrained some of my theologian's instincts to pester Paul about one pet topic or another and instead just let him say what he wanted to say.

And our conversation has been quite different. I have heard in Paul's letter his love for his dear friends, and, through Paul's loving words, I have encountered God's love.

In this reading, grace has grown bigger, judgement is more real, yet mercy is warmer. God's freedom is grander, my hope is firmer and God's peace is fuller.

My prayer each day as I wrote this guide was that it really would be useful.

Chapter 2 lays out the things that are useful to know before you start reading Romans. It includes a summary of the 'ancient mystery' in the Hebrew scriptures that Paul keeps referring back to. Don't skip that bit. It really is useful for understanding where Paul is coming from and what he's trying to get at.

Chapter 3 charts a path through Romans and then walks with you stage by stage. It should be useful in helping you think about what Paul was thinking about. His thoughts are grand and glorious – they could not be otherwise; he's been tasked with writing about God's grace and righteousness – but the guide should help explain what Paul means. Along the way, I also keep connecting each part of Romans with others. There really is a flow to Paul's argument in this letter, and those connections are useful in helping us sense that.

Chapter 4 compares Romans with others of the earliest Jewish-Christian writings collected in the New Testament. Some of you may be interested in sorting out the tension between Paul and James on faith and justification. You can find their discussion there.

Finally, chapter 5 reflects on ways that Paul's message in Romans continues to speak to us today. 'Us', of course, depends on who you are. I hope my comments connect usefully with you where you are. If they don't, do listen to the Spirit as you read and pray and also talk with others. He knows you best of all.

With God's help, this really will be a useful guide to Romans. May you find it so. And may it lead you, with Paul, through his grand letter right up to its majestic conclusion.

To the only wise God be glory forever through Jesus Christ! Amen.
ROMANS 16:27

Ernest
Bengaluru, India

2

Start here

Sometime around AD57, a Jew named Paul wrote a letter in Greek and sent it from Corinth, in southern Greece, to a group of his close friends and their associates in Rome. The letter was carried by Phoebe, a deacon from the church at nearby Cenchreae, whom Paul called 'sister' and who had also been his patron. The letter crossed a sea and journeyed up a peninsula, and it was read, we may suppose, with the warmth and interest recipients would show who knew its sender variously as beloved and son, co-worker and teacher.

A letter was delivered, but a legacy had begun. Over other seas, through other lands, across 2,000 years and in even more languages, it continued to speak and to speak meaningfully. It has confounded and converted, instructed and encouraged with the same enduring significance that led its early readers to recognise it, in 2 Peter's words, as 'scripture', a prophecy spoken from God as the Holy Spirit carried the person along (2 Peter 1:20–21; 3:15–16). Here, in Paul's words to his 'brothers and sisters' in Rome, readers have found God's words to his beloved ones in every age and place.

Paul's brothers and sisters in Rome

To read Romans well, then, it is useful to start with knowing who Paul's brothers and sisters in Rome were.

1 **They were Paul's friends.** Though Paul had not yet visited them in Rome, he knew many of them from elsewhere. Epenetus, Ampliatus, Stachys and Persis were beloved 'dear friends' of his. Rufus' mother was a mother to Paul as well (16:5–13).

    Paul's relationship with the people to whom he wrote set the tone for the letter. From the opening words to the closing, Paul, though bold, is neither alarmed nor angry. Instead, he is filled with love for his dear friends (1:7; 15:14; 16:20).

To all in Rome who are loved by God and called to be his holy people: Grace and peace to you… The grace of our Lord Jesus be with you.
ROMANS 1:7; 16:20

2. **They were maturing believers,** people whose trust in God directed their attitudes and actions in everyday life. Through this faith, God had made them replete with goodness and 'filled with knowledge' (15:14). Some of them had used this knowledge to teach others: Priscilla (also called Prisca), Aquila and Urbanus had been Paul's 'fellow workers in Christ'. And Andronicus and Junia were apostles (16:3, 7, 9).

   In light of their faithful character, Paul assumed at least two things when he wrote to them. First, he assumed that they were oriented on God, that they wanted to love God and do good (15:14). Second, Paul assumed that they knew Israel's scriptures, especially Moses' law (7:1). (The section below on 'Disclosing the ancient mystery' on page 21 below outlines some of the things Paul and his friends knew from the scriptures.)

3. **They were people God loved.** This is the starting point of Paul's correspondence, how he addresses them in the opening of the letter. And it is the foundation of Paul's argument: God knew them and loved them first. God is their father; they are his beloved children and each other's beloved brothers and sisters. For Paul, this love of God for his

children is the source of the grace, righteousness, mercy and holiness that he will discuss throughout the letter (5:1–11; 8:28–39). And it is this same love that draws us across two millennia into reading Paul's letter to his beloved brothers and sisters as God's letter to us, his beloved children (see 4:23–24; 15:4–6).

4 **They were called to be holy.** This is the ending point of Paul's correspondence. Beginning with the identity his dear friends already have as God's loved ones, Paul wrote the letter to urge them to live as God's holy ones. They are called to be holy, to belong in a special way to God rather than to their age. And they are called to serve God in a special way, much as Moses' law instructed priests and temple servants to serve God (12:1; 15:16–21).

Next, to appreciate Paul's friends' life as a group, a short history of the church in Rome is useful.

The church in Rome

From the very first day – when the Holy Spirit came down like fire and wind from heaven – the new Jesus movement included residents from Rome. Roman

'Jews and converts to Judaism' had gone on pilgrimage to Jerusalem for the annual festival of Pentecost (Acts 2:1–11). There, just a few days after Jesus was taken into heaven, they heard his follower Peter testify that God had raised Jesus up and exalted him to his right hand. This was evidence, Peter concluded confidently, that God had made Jesus 'both Lord and Messiah' (Acts 1:6–11; 2:22–36).

We may assume that some of these visitors from Rome were among the 3,000 that day who accepted Peter's message and were baptised (Acts 2:37–42). They would have returned eventually to Rome and continued attending synagogue on sabbath. There they would have heard Moses' law read and taught (Acts 15:21).

It is likely that they also began to gather as people who followed Jesus. In time, other believers would have joined them, both Jews and non-Jews. At some point, Paul's relatives Andronicus and Junia, two distinguished apostles (sent either by Jesus after his resurrection or by a church as their messengers), arrived (Romans 16:7). By the time Paul wrote them in 57, the brothers and sisters in Rome were assembling in Priscilla and Aquila's house and probably also in Aristobulus' and Narcissus' homes (16:5, 10, 11).

But the church's story was not one of undisturbed growth. Eight years earlier, in 49, Emperor Claudius had expelled Jews from the city of Rome. They were, according to the historian Suetonius, constantly agitated about someone named Chrestus (*Claudius* 25; see Acts 18:2).

While Jews, like Aquila and Priscilla, were absent, the gathering of believers would, naturally, have become less Jewish in character. And when the Jewish believers returned, as Priscilla and Aquila did, the difference was evident and tension mounted. Some ate only meat that Moses' law prescribed as clean; others ate only vegetables, perhaps because meat was often dedicated to an idol before it was sold in the market; and others ate any food. Some observed one day as special; others treated all days the same (14:1–23). Some boasted about having Moses' law; others were inclined to ignore it (2:17–24; 6:15—7:6). To these dear brothers and sisters in this situation at this time, Paul writes Romans.

Romans itself is both a profound theological treatise and a warm pastoral letter – it is also a frank apostolic appeal for support. The following sections outline these several factors that formed the letter: Paul's practical concerns for his brothers and sisters, his proposed apostolic trip to Spain, the deep theological themes that inform his message and the grand historical panorama that sets everything in perspective.

Paul's main concerns

Paul had at least three main concerns as he wrote to God's loved ones.

1 **There were rifts within God's 'household'.** Some people were haughty, thinking more highly of themselves than they ought. People judged and despised each other from opposite sides of the same issue. Competition elbowed cooperation aside; the desire to please themselves got in the way of building their neighbours up. Some people were offensive and divisive. Love's generous acceptance and enduring peace had been curtailed (2:1–5; 12:1—15:13).

2 **Non-Jews and Jews (and perhaps people who called themselves Jews) disagreed about what it meant to be God's children.** Who are God's children? Who are the people who receive God's special blessings because they are Abraham's children (4:1–25)? Are God's people still under Moses' law

(2:12–29; 6:1–7:25; 13:8–10)? Should they eat meat only from clean animals, honour the sabbath and observe other festivals (14:1–23)? Should males be circumcised (2:25–29; 4:9–12)? If God's people don't obey the whole of God's law, will God still consider them righteous?

3 **God's children were struggling against sin and the flesh.** Some of them may have given in to the self-centred desires the flesh has for quarrelling, jealousy and debauchery (13:13–14). Others wanted to do good, but they found themselves inevitably doing just the opposite. Their inner selves – which 'delighted in God's law' – were waylaid by weak bodies that sin had occupied, and they were miserable (7:5–25).

These concerns filled Paul's heart as he wrote to his friends in Rome. But why was he writing just then?

Paul's desire to share a gift with his friends

Paul wrote to his friends in Rome at this point because he planned to visit them after some time. As Christ Jesus' minister to non-Jewish nations, Paul had proclaimed 'the gospel of Christ' as far as Illyricum (modern-day Bosnia and Herzegovina). He now proposed, after a trip to Jerusalem, to travel further west to Spain, where the good news that Jesus is king had not yet been announced. Along the way, Paul wanted to visit the brothers and sisters in Rome and be refreshed in their company. He would, God willing, come with joy and with Christ's blessing, share a spiritual gift with them that would strengthen them and be encouraged in return by their faith. He also wanted them to send him on to Spain (1:10–15; 15:22–33).

That was the occasion for Paul's letter to God's loved ones in Rome. Yet how incongruous it seems! First, because Paul's plans did not play out as he had hoped. Three years would pass before Paul reached Rome – and that in chains, to be tried in Caesar's court. Nevertheless (or perhaps, all the more) the sight of his brothers and sisters would still be a cause for thanksgiving and a source of courage (Acts 28:14–31).

The occasion – and the concerns – also seem awkwardly insignificant when compared with the magnificence of the letter they gave rise to. Only about five percent of the book of Romans relates directly to Paul's proposed ministry. And if the real issues were those listed above, would not the inspiring principles in chapter 12 and the practical instructions in chapters 13 to 15 have sufficed?

But Paul was doing more. In this letter he was sharing a spiritual gift that would strengthen his brothers' and sisters' faith. And, typical of Paul, he was giving them much more to think about than simply telling them what to do. Paul was proclaiming God's good news about his Son. He was explaining its themes: God's righteousness and faithfulness, grace, power and love. And he was calling his brothers and sisters to heed his message, to believe and to live and serve as God's holy people.

The gospel of God – the gospel… regarding his Son, who as to his earthly life was a descendant of David, and who through the Spirit of holiness was appointed the Son of God in power by his resurrection from the dead: Jesus Christ our Lord. Through him we received grace and apostleship to call all the Gentiles to the obedience that comes from faith for his name's sake… To all in Rome who are loved by God and called to be his holy people: Grace and peace to you from God our Father and from the Lord Jesus Christ.
ROMANS 1:1–5, 7

Romans' message: God's good news about his Son, Jesus Christ our Lord

Paul states the message of his letter right at the beginning: this letter is about God's 'gospel' or good news. That good news is:

God's Son Jesus, whom God raised from the dead, is King and Lord, and he calls all nations to believe him for his name's sake.

This is a message of grace and peace: God seeks reconciliation with sinners, and he sets them right and makes them truly alive through faith.

And this message shows how ancient promises, hidden mysteriously in the prophetic writings, had now come true in the life, death, resurrection and reign of the Lord Jesus Christ. Thus, most useful of all for reading Paul's letter to his friends in Rome is seeing this 'story' from his perspective.

Disclosing the ancient mystery

The people and parts of a story make sense within their own story; outside of it, they don't. It makes sense for three children to dress in bathrobes and walk across a stage (as solemnly as they can) to give gold, frankincense and myrrh to a doll in a feed trough. But it would make no sense at all if one of them wore a red suit stuffed with pillows and shouted, 'Ho, ho, ho! Merry Christmas!' However much we may want to jump to the fun bit where Father Christmas gives us presents, he simply doesn't fit in that story.

Nor, frankly, will many of our modern assumptions about God, the world or religion make much sense if we shove them into Paul's ancient story.

The following six sections summarise how Paul's knowledgeable friends might instruct us in the ancient mystery hidden in the prophetic writings.

Creation and humans, sin and decay

The eternal God created all things. He made human persons and shared his glory with them so that they would serve him by extending the blessing of his good rule to all creation (1:20; see Genesis 1:26–31). But the first human (*adam* is the Hebrew word for 'human person') chose himself over God and fell short of that glorious charge. Through his sin, death entered the world (3:23; 5:12–19; see Genesis 3).

At that time, God subjected creation to futility and decay. Since then, creation has waited in hope for God's children to be revealed, for those children will live up to God's glory and bring creation into their freedom (8:18–22; see Genesis 3:17–19).

All humans too are enslaved, by sin. Indeed, God has locked them inside disobedience, but he has done so in order that he might have mercy on them all (3:9–23; 11:32).

Abraham

From among all human families, God made a covenant – he committed himself to a relationship – with one: Abraham, along with his wife Sarah and their descendants (Romans 4). When God promised Abraham, who was childless, many descendants, Abraham believed God, and God counted Abraham's faith as righteousness (Genesis 15). Through their family, God promised to bless all other families on earth (Genesis 12:1–3). Indeed, Abraham would become the 'father of many nations' and inherit the earth (Genesis 17:1–8).

The law

Several hundred years later, God gave his law through the prophet Moses to the descendants of Abraham's grandson Jacob, renamed 'Israel'. This law set for God's people a pattern of a just and good life. It instructed them not to covet but to love their neighbours as themselves (7:7–12; 13:8–10; see Exodus 20:1–17; Leviticus 19:18).

It was a 'holy' law. First, the law detailed a holy liturgy for Israel's priests to follow in worshipping God. Some animal sacrifices were for sin; the animal's blood covered over (or atoned for) the people's sin (3:24–26; 8:3; see Leviticus 1; 4:1—6:7; 16). Other sacrifices celebrated the peace and fellowship that people enjoyed with God after he saved them from something (12:1; see Leviticus 3).

Second, the law detailed a holy lifestyle for Israel's people (Romans 14). It set a calendar of weekly sabbaths and annual festivals for the people to honour their relationship with the Lord (Leviticus 23). It prohibited the worship of images (Exodus 20:4–6). It identified the meat of some animals as clean and of others as unclean (Leviticus 11). And it affirmed God's command to Abraham that all males should be circumcised (Leviticus 12:3; see Genesis 17). These and other practices set Israel apart from the other 'nations' as holy. English versions often translate this word 'Gentiles', from the Latin word *gentilis*, 'of a family or nation'. Paul and other Jews just called them 'foreskins' (3:30).

David

After Israel settled in the land, God made a covenant with their second king, David the son of Jesse, and promised him an eternal dynasty. For generation after generation, the son would be anointed and made king. God also promised to adopt each of David's successors as his son (1:3; see 2 Samuel 7:8–16).

The prophetic writings

Later prophets reflected on God's promises to Abraham and David (15:8–21). They foresaw God's people singing God's praises among other nations, as David did (2 Samuel 22:50). They called those nations to join the praise (Psalm 117). And they anticipated that when the anointed one, David's descendant, began to rule – with justice and mercy – the nations would hope in him (Isaiah 11:10). Indeed, nations who had never heard would see and understand (Isaiah 52:15). They, as priests, would offer their lives to God as holy sacrifices (Isaiah 66:20–21). And God would call people from among the Jews and the other nations to be his people, the children he loves (9:23–26; see Hosea 1:10; 2:23).

However, the prophets also rebuked Israel for their obstinate disobedience (10:21; see Isaiah 65:2). Many found that the law, far from enabling them to follow the holy lifestyle it prescribed, actually prompted them to more frequent lapses and showed that their repeated errors were genuinely sinful (5:20; 7:5–13).

On Paul's reading, the law had taught Israel to believe (10:6-10). In Moses' last words to Israel, he said, 'What I am commanding you today is not too difficult for you or beyond your reach… No, the word is very near you; it is in your mouth and in your heart so that you may obey it' (Deuteronomy 30:11, 14). Yet Israel missed the point, for they pursued righteousness as though it were something they could attain by simply *doing* the law without trusting God (9:30—10:5). As a result, according to Paul, many Jews were little better than non-Jews (2:17—3:23).

Paul

This story and its plotline were a chart and compass for Paul. The scriptures identified both the human problem of sin – common to Jews and all other nations – and also the inability of Moses' law to make people good. The law and the prophets foreshadowed a blood offering that would cover over sins. They promised forgiveness, righteousness and salvation for everyone who called on the Lord's name in faith. They foretold a kingdom in which a descendant of Abraham would inherit the world and a son of David would rule all nations. They described Adam's children gloriously alive, serving God and blessing creation. And they foresaw God's final judgement when every knee would bend and every tongue acknowledge God.

All this Paul believed to be true, really true. In line with this story, Paul charted the course of his own apostolic ministry – to the nations, westward round the Mediterranean. This story mapped out his world view: the way he saw God, the Son and the Spirit, all humans and God's children. It plotted out how things had been, how they had changed recently and what they would become. And it showed him the true north of faithfulness, righteousness, love and holiness. That's why – for these reasons and many others – this story is the most useful thing to know before you read Romans.

A few words about words

Finally, to understand Romans as Paul intended, it's useful to recognise the members of two key groups of words in Greek. The terms in each group hold together easily in Greek, but the connections might not be so obvious in English.

The fundamental concept 'faith' (*pistis*) can be translated 'trust' or 'belief'. Likewise:

- believe (*pisteuo*) appears as 'trust', 'entrust' or 'have faith'
- unfaithfulness (*apistia*) as 'faithlessness', 'unbelief' or 'distrust'.

Second, the significant term 'righteousness' (*dikaiosyne*) may also be translated 'justice' or 'fairness'. Likewise:

- righteous (*dikaios*) appears as 'just' or 'upright'
- unrighteousness (*adikia*) as 'injustice', 'unfairness', 'sinfulness', 'wickedness' or 'evil'

- unrighteous (*adikos*) as 'unjust' or 'unfair'
- righteous act (*dikaioma*) as 'righteous [or] just requirement [or] decree', 'justice', 'judgement' or 'justification'
- declare righteous (*dikaioo*) as 'justify', 'prove [or] make right' or 'set free'
- justification (*dikaiosis*) as 'right relationship'.

Recognising the words in these two families is useful because Paul keeps using them to piece the bits of his argument together into a whole.

3

Guide to the contents

Two outlines: the path and the steps

Romans is a letter. Like any letter, it has an opening and a closing. But, in the case of this letter, that opening and closing are wrapped around content that is truly glorious: complex argument thick with citations, here perplexing, there inspiring. Along the way it is easy to lose one's way in the wood, to forget that **Paul is writing to people God loves about God's good news about Jesus Christ and about what it means to be Jesus' holy people**. Two outlines should be useful guides: the first shows the whole path; the second points out the steps along the way.

The path of Paul's argument

- Paul greets his friends with God's good news, 1:1–17

Guide to the contents 31

- The faithful and righteous God condemns sin but sets believers right, 1:18—4:25. *Oh, that's wonderfully generous! So how should we live now?*
- The Son and the Spirit enable believers to live right, 5:1—8:39. *Will they really? Hasn't God defaulted on his promises to his people Israel?*
- God has been and will be faithful to Israel, 9:1—11:36. *Ah, I hadn't seen it that way. So what again about us now?*
- Paul calls believers to holiness and love, 12:1—15:13. *Of course, that is only appropriate and, indeed, what we want most.*
- Paul plans an apostolic visit to Rome, 15:14-33
- Paul blesses his friends, 16:1-27

The steps along the way

- Paul greets his friends with God's good news, 1:1-17
  - Paul writes about the gospel to God's loved ones in Rome, 1:1-7
  - Paul is thankful for his friends' faith and wants to visit them, 1:8-15
  - God's gospel reveals faith, righteousness and life, 1:16-17

- The faithful and righteous God condemns sin but sets believers right, 1:18—4:25
  - God is angry about people's wickedness, 1:18-32
  - God will repay each person according to their actions, 2:1-11
  - God judges everyone's thoughts and actions, whether Jew or not, 2:12-29
  - God's words are still special, reliable and right, 3:1-8
  - The law shows that everyone – Jew or Greek – is 'under sin', 3:9-20
  - But, since God presented Jesus' blood as a sacrifice that covers sin, God is right when he sets believers right, 3:21-31
  - Faith is the essential element in the promise to Abraham and his many heirs, 4:1-25

- The Son and the Spirit enable believers to live right, 5:1—8:39
  - Through Jesus' death, the God who loves us has made peace with us, 5:1-11
  - God's grace – and Jesus' righteous act – are greater than sin and death, 5:12-21
  - Baptised people share Jesus' experience of dying to sin and coming alive to God, 6:1-14

- So believers should present their bodies to God to do right and become holy, 6:15-23
- Since Jesus died, the believers are not bound by Moses' law; now the Spirit makes them alive, 7:1-6
- Moses' law, although holy, could not cure sin's infection in my weak body, 7:7-25
- But the Spirit enables Jesus' people to live right as God's children, 8:1-17
- God always loves his children – however grim their circumstances – and he will make them glorious, 8:18-39

- God has been and will be faithful to Israel, 9:1—11:36
  - God's word to Israel didn't fail; God's people are those he chooses to have mercy on, 9:1-29
  - Many within Israel didn't know that God's righteousness comes from faith, not from actions, 9:30—10:21
  - God has mercy on disobedient people: some from Israel and the nations now, all Israel eventually, 11:1-36

- Paul calls believers to holiness and love, 12:1—15:13

- Since God has been so compassionate, offer him your bodies and let him renew your mind, 12:1–2
- By faith, build a good, loving and peaceable community, 12:3–21
- Comply with civil authorities, 13:1–7
- Love each other – that satisfies the whole point of Moses' law, 13:8–10
- Act the part of Jesus, and don't make plans for what your flesh wants, 13:11–14
- Accept the Lord's people, whatever their habits, 14:1—15:6
- The nations will praise Christ their Lord, just as God promised, 15:7–13

- Paul plans an apostolic visit to Rome, 15:14–33

- Paul blesses his friends, 16:1–27
  - Paul greets and encourages his friends, 16:1–23
  - Paul praises God for bringing the nations to obedient faith, 16:25–27

With these two guides in hand, let's walk the path through Romans in stages and note important features along the way.

Paul greets his friends with God's good news, 1:1–17

Paul opens his letter directly and gets straight to its main theme: God's good news (1:1). In the verses that follow, he summarises God's good news about his Son Jesus (1:2–6), greets his friends (1:7), says how much he wants to visit them (1:8–15) and returns again to his main theme (1:16–17).

Paul writes about the gospel to God's loved ones in Rome, 1:1–7

Paul packs these opening paragraphs with the main theme of his letter and with many of the **key words** he will use again and again.

Christ Jesus called Paul and charged him to proclaim God's good news (or, in older English, his **gospel**). In Paul's world, good news usually announced the reign of a new monarch. Paul too is announcing the reign of a new king: God's Son Jesus.

However, the news is not new. For centuries prior, God had sent word through his prophets, promising, however cryptically, a king like this.

The king's name is *Iesous* (**Jesus**), the Greek rendition of Joshua, Israel's first leader in the land. A few of Paul's readers may have known its meaning in Hebrew: 'Yahweh [*yaho*] is salvation [*shua*]'.

According to his human lineage, this Jesus was known to be descended from David, the ancient king of Israel to whom God had promised an eternal dynasty (2 Samuel 7:8–16). Thus, when Paul identifies Jesus as a descendant of King David and calls him *christos* (the Greek word for '**anointed**'), he is claiming that Jesus is the rightful heir to that throne, that kingdom and those promises (1:1–2).

Paul also identifies Jesus the anointed as **God's Son** (1:3–4). According to the Spirit of holiness, Jesus was distinguished as God's Son in power when he rose from the dead. God promised David to adopt each of David's successors as his son (2 Samuel 7:14). But all previous sons-of-David–sons-of-God had died. By rising from the dead, this anointed son of David was distinguished as God's Son in power, one who was already God's Son before he was sent to become human (8:3; 9:5).

For Paul, finally, God's Son in power, Jesus the anointed King, is also worthy of the title '**Lord**' (1:4).

He is not only 'our' Lord – Lord of those who serve him – but also Lord of the Jews, Lord of all nations and Lord of the dead and the living. Indeed, he is the one that Israel's scriptures call 'Lord': *Yahweh*, the Being One (1:4; 9:5; 10:12; 14:9, 11; 15:11).

According to the prophetic writings, the Davidic kingdom would eventually rule other nations. So the new King Jesus appointed Paul ambassador to the nations, and Paul travelled from nation to nation announcing Jesus' reign. Paul called those nations to 'the obedience that comes from **faith**' (1:5). He urged them to believe his message, to acknowledge Jesus as King and Lord and to obey Jesus faithfully (1:1–6).

'You too are called,' Paul tells his readers. You are people God **loves** already, and he calls you to be **holy**.

'Grace and peace to you,' Paul writes, combining traditional Greek and Jewish greetings. **Grace** is God's gift to them, an expression of his own kindness and favour. **Peace** comes from being reconciled with God (they had been God's enemies), which then leads on to peace with each other.

Paul is thankful for his friends' faith and wants to visit them, 1:8–15

With many of his key concepts in place, Paul addresses God's loved ones in Rome directly: I thank God for you and your faith, and I pray for you without a break.

Paul is also keen to visit them. He plans to share a spiritual gift with them, expounding further the good news that he will set forth in this letter. And he wants them to aid him in his journey onward to Spain (15:22–33). As they share these gifts and others with each other, they will be 'encouraged by each other's faith' (1:11–13). Here and throughout the letter, faith – genuine trust and trustworthiness – is the ubiquitous string that Paul uses again and again to tie the parts of his argument together and make it work – as he does in the next two sentences.

God's gospel reveals faith, righteousness and life, 1:16–17

For I am not ashamed of the gospel, because it is the power of God that brings salvation to everyone who believes: first to the Jew, then to the Gentile. For in

the gospel the righteousness of God is revealed – a righteousness that is by faith from first to last, just as it is written: 'The righteous will live by faith.'
ROMANS 1:16–17

Paul's good news is rather fantastical. He asserts that a man from the long-defunct royal family of an inconsequential province has come back to life and now, as alleged 'Son of God', claims the allegiance of all nations. And Paul dares to put that in a letter to residents of the empire's capital city! But Paul is not ashamed.

Paul is not ashamed because this good news about Jesus is God's right and effective way to save everyone who believes.

Here – and for the next ten chapters – the two important word groups of faith and righteousness come together. God is **faithful**. He is reliable. He keeps his promises, even the promises to Israel, which he seems to have broken. And, in his faithfulness, God is **righteous**: he is faithful both to his righteous character and to his righteous covenants, the relationships he promised his people.

Paul's letter shows God's righteousness in three ways. First, God is rightly angry about human unrighteousness (1:18).

But, second, true to his righteous character and covenant, God will save his people from the judgement they deserve. Here, God's faithfulness shows itself in both mercy and justice. God presented his Son Jesus as an offering to cover sins; so when ungodly people trust him, he forgives their sins and counts them as righteous (3:21—4:8).

Third, God's righteousness is seen in the lives of his children. God's Spirit makes believers truly alive with Jesus so that they can live right (6:1—8:17).

From beginning to end, then, God's righteousness is connected to faithfulness and faith.

Throughout this letter, when Paul needs evidence to support one of his claims, he turns to Israel's scriptures. Here he quotes from the prophet Habakkuk. In that ancient scroll, Habakkuk complains that wicked people in the kingdom of Judah are oppressing the righteous (Habakkuk 1:1–4). In reply, the Lord promises Habakkuk that he will judge the wicked and rescue the righteous in Judah. However, he will, astonishingly, use the 'ruthless' Babylonian army to do so. 'But', the Lord promises Habakkuk, 'the righteous person will live by his faithfulness' (2:4).

That one sentence is the ideal starting point for Paul's argument because its words connect three of his major themes: righteousness, faith and life. It's useful also because, in Paul's phrasing, its meaning is ambiguous. Is it the person who is righteous from faith who will live? Is it that the righteous person has faithful faith and so will live? Or is it that God will be faithful to ensure that the righteous person lives? 'Yes,' Paul would say.

These three concepts are too intertwined to be separated out. And they are all faithful and righteous expressions of the living God's love for his people.

The faithful and righteous God condemns sin but sets believers right, 1:18—4:25

God's righteousness is not his only attitude that is revealed. His anger is also revealed.

God is angry about people's wickedness, 1:18–32

From the beginning, Paul argues, humans have understood that an eternal, powerful God made the cosmos they see. However, they responded to this knowledge by orienting themselves not on God's greatness or goodness, but on their own ends.

The consequence was a steady decline into impiety, unrighteousness and evil. At each step, selfish thoughts or motives expressed themselves in sinful actions that only degraded them further.

- Their hearts' thoughts were foolish, and they worshipped images.
- Their hearts' desires for impurity led them to degrade 'their bodies with one another'.
- God gave them over to a degrading mood or passion. They let go of the relationship that is 'natural' for men and women and burned with desire for people of their own sex.
- In sum, 'a depraved mind' led them both to do and to champion every kind of 'evil, greed and depravity'.

Just as they did not think it worth while to retain the knowledge of God, so God gave them over to a depraved mind, so that they do what ought not to be done.
ROMANS 1:28

It may sound as though Paul is writing about the other nations – and he is – but Israel's prophets (from Isaiah to Malachi) had long made it clear that many in Israel were as bad as the nations around them (2:21).

The path of Paul's argument starts here: God is rightly angry that humans have spurned him and debased themselves and are destroying each other.

God will repay each person according to their actions, 2:1–11

Of course, few people see themselves as evil as Paul describes the world's peoples. Some among the brothers and sisters in Rome saw themselves as better than others, whom they judged for doing what they thought was bad (Romans 14).

'But you're inexcusable,' Paul writes – to no one in particular, though many someones will feel his point particularly – 'because you do the same thing.'

Paul will address *you* many times throughout this letter. This method allows him to present his argument simply and clearly, as though it were a conversation. Of course, it will be important to discern whether the words we are reading are Paul representing his own ideas or Paul putting words in the mouth of a *you* or a *someone*.

At this point in the letter, the person is judging others for doing what they too do. But the person is misreading the situation. God has not yet responded to the situation, because he is willing to wait. This, then, is not the time to fill the gap and judge someone (though God does appoint some humans to do so for him, 13:1–6). Rather, it is an opportunity to think again about your own way of living.

For God will judge, Paul warns. As both an ancient psalm (Psalm 62) and a proverb (Proverbs 24:12) say, God 'will repay each person according to what they have done' (Romans 2:6).

There will be trouble and distress for every human being who does evil… but glory, honour and peace for everyone who does good.
ROMANS 2:9–10

And, as Paul insists, God will not show special favour to one group of people over the others.

But does God judge someone's faith or their actions?

If it is through faith that people are saved from God's appropriate anger against their sin, how then does God consider people's actions when he judges them?

That question bears pondering. So this guide won't answer it straightway. Rather, as we walk together through Paul's letter, keep asking it, especially when we get to Romans 8.

And pay special attention when he writes the following. (You can also peak ahead to what the guide will say at those points.)

- When someone believes God, God forgives their sins and counts their faith as righteousness (4:5–8).
- As believers have been declared righteous because of Jesus' blood, so too, through Jesus, they will be saved from God's righteous anger (5:9–11).
- So there is no condemnation for those who are 'in' Christ Jesus. At no point – even in the

judgement – can anything separate them from God's love for them (8:1, 31–39).
- God's Spirit makes God's children truly alive. He enables them to do with their bodies the good things they desire in their hearts (6:17—8:17).
- As God's Spirit renews their minds, God's children are able to discern God's good will: that they love good and do good (12:1–2, 9, 21; 13:3–4).
- In these ways, they are replete with goodness, and they live up to the human person's glorious calling to bring the blessing of God's good rule to all of creation (3:23; 8:18–21; 15:14).
- From beginning to end, all of this is an expression of the faithful and righteous God's mercy, his love for his children. And so all of this is for his glory (1:16–17; 11:36—12:2).

God judges everyone's thoughts and actions, whether Jew or not, 2:12–29

When it comes to God's judgement, there is no special advantage in being a Jew, because **it's not ancestry or appearances that God judges, but actions**.

To make his point, Paul contrasts two different sorts of people: (1) those who have Moses' law but don't 'do' it, and (2) those who don't have Moses' law but do 'do' it.

Of course, there are also people who have the law and do it (see Zechariah and Elizabeth in Luke 1:6) and people who don't have the law and don't do it (see the nations in Ephesians 4:17).

On the one hand is another *you*, someone who calls themselves a Jew. Such a person boasts about being instructed by the law, the very 'embodiment of knowledge and truth' (2:17–20). But, Paul says, you break the law you boast in, and you dishonour the God who gave it to you (2:23).

On the other hand, there are non-Jews who do what the law prescribes. They do so because the law's instructions are written on their hearts (2:13–15). Through the prophet Jeremiah God had promised to write his law on the Israelites' hearts (Jeremiah 31:33). And through Ezekiel God had said he would give them a new, sensitive heart (Ezekiel 36:26–27). And now, the assortment of believers in Rome includes non-Jews who have received God's love in their hearts and are obeying him from their hearts (5:5; 6:17).

What matters, then – what God assesses – is not public appearance, but a devoted heart that expresses itself in diligent obedience.

So those who call themselves 'Jews' are not actually better than the people they feel superior to (2:17–24). Even the sign of circumcision that points to their special relationship with God is ambivalent. A sign is a good and useful thing. But if the thing the sign points to isn't actually there, the sign is pointless (2:25–27).

A person is a Jew who is one inwardly; and circumcision is circumcision of the heart, by the Spirit, not by the written code. Such a person's praise is not from other people, but from God.
ROMANS 2:29

Taking up a metaphor from Moses, Paul describes such a heart as 'circumcised': it is sensitive because the callus that surrounded it has been cut away. Moses told Israel they must circumcise their own hearts, for such hearts are receptive to the deep virtues the law instils: love and godly fear (Deuteronomy 10:12–16). Now God's Spirit has circumcised their hearts, just as Moses promised he would (Deuteronomy 30:1–11). That is real circumcision, Paul says, and those are real Jews. God accepts, and even praises, them (2:28–29).

God's words are still special, reliable and right, 3:1–8

'So is there no special advantage in being a Jew or in being circumcised?' the other person asks, rejoining the conversation. They are certainly aware of tensions, among the believers in Rome, between non-Jews and those who call themselves Jews.

PAUL   There are many advantages. The Jews have God's own oracles.

PERSON   But what if they were unfaithful with them?

PAUL   God is still faithful. His words are true. And his righteous judgement of unrighteousness is actually honourable.

PERSON   But if God is somehow honoured by our unrighteousness, how is it right for God to be angry with us?

PAUL   Don't get distracted.

The law shows that everyone – Jew or Greek – is 'under sin', 3:9–20

PERSON   To the point then: has the advantage of having God's oracles (and circumcision) helped us Jews attain some special standing before God?

PAUL   Never ever!

For we have already made the charge that Jews and Gentiles alike are all under the power of sin.
ROMANS 3:9

To support his claim, Paul quotes from 'the law': the Hebrew scriptures generally: six songs attributed to King David (Psalms 5, 10, 14, 36, 53 and 140) and three lines from Isaiah (Isaiah 59:7–8). Psalm 14 heads the list well. There God surveys all of Adam's children – not just the other 'wicked' nations – and concludes, In thought, in motive and in action, 'There is no one righteous, not even one' (see Romans 3:10–12).

The scriptures that follow show how sin's infection – beginning with people's thoughts, motives and actions in their centre – has spread to their parts: throats, tongues, lips, mouths, feet and eyes (3:13–18).

PAUL   And, since those passages are from 'the law', we know they are speaking to Jews. So Jews' mouths are shut too. God will hold the whole world accountable. As I said above:

All who sin apart from the law will also perish apart from the law, and all who sin under the law will be judged by the law.
ROMANS 2:12

'Therefore,' Paul concludes, quoting another Davidic psalm, 'no one will be declared righteous in God's sight' by pursuing the law's actions (3:20; see Psalm 143:2).

But, since God presented Jesus' blood as a sacrifice that covers sin, God is right when he sets believers right, 3:21–31

Paul's account of God's good news has started with grim news. To restate two points: (1) God made humans in his image and charged them to extend the blessing of his good rule to the world, but they – both the first and all since – sinned and fell short of this glorious role (3:23); and (2) in a sort of truce, God overlooked their sins (3:25; see 2:4).

'But now,' Paul says, 'God's righteousness has been disclosed' (3:21). The ancient Hebrew scriptures testified to this righteousness, but it was disclosed only in Paul's lifetime: in Jesus' death.

All are justified freely by his grace through the redemption that came by Christ Jesus. God presented Christ as a sacrifice of atonement, through the shedding of his blood.
ROMANS 3:24–25

God's action fulfilled in a dramatic way what the rites on the Day of Atonement (Yom Kippur) had foreshadowed. In that autumn ceremony, the high priest slaughtered a goat as a sacrifice for sin. He then took its blood into the holiest room of the sanctuary and sprinkled it on the cover of the golden box, in which the copies of God's covenant with Israel were kept. By this solemn ritual, the high priest covered over the many ways the people's sins had damaged their covenanted relationship with God (Leviticus 16:15–17).

Now, like the high priest, God has presented Christ Jesus as both the cover on the ark of the covenant and the blood sprinkled on it. Jesus was faithful to the point of death; his blood covers over the many ways everyone's sins have damaged their relationship with God (Romans 3:22, 25). This extraordinary ritual demonstrates God's righteousness (3:26).

Now that God has shown his righteousness in that way, his righteousness is also disclosed when, in his generous kindness, he declares righteous everyone who believes in Jesus. He forgives their sins and ransoms them from their consequences (3:26).

PAUL So where then is any boasting about having God's law? [See 2:17–23.]

PERSON I suppose it's ruled out.

PAUL Through which way of approaching the law?

PERSON By trying to practise the many things the law requires?

PAUL No, by obeying the law's command to believe. For God justifies someone because of faith, not because of the law's practices. Unless you think God is only the

God of the Jews, to whom he gave the law. Isn't he the God of the other nations too?

PERSON He must be the God of all the nations, since there is only one God.

PAUL Exactly. And he will declare the circumcised man right by faith and the 'foreskin' right through that same faith.

PERSON But doesn't this 'faith' nullify the law?

PAUL Never ever! Rather, by faith we are upholding the law.

Faith is the essential element in God's promise about Abraham and his many heirs, 4:1–25

At first, it seems as though this next step in Paul's argument (chapter 4) will simply be proof that, indeed, righteousness is God's gift in response to faith.

PERSON Yes, but what about Abraham, the first father of the Jews? Was he declared righteous because of his actions or because of his faith?

PAUL   What does the scripture say?

Abraham believed God, and it was credited to him as righteousness.
ROMANS 4:3 (see GENESIS 15:6)

This declaration – and the forgiveness it entails – is the happiest of news, as Abraham's descendant David observed (Romans 4:6–8). And Abraham received it not after he had been circumcised, but (shudder) while he still had a foreskin (4:9–11)!

How strange! We are accustomed to associating righteousness with the actions of Abraham and his circumcised family, but it's actually quite in keeping with the example of Abraham for God to declare impious, uncircumcised people righteous when they believe (4:5, 9–12).

And when God speaks, his word is powerful. He 'calls into being things that were not' (4:17).

For example, even when Abraham had no offspring, God promised Abraham and his offspring 'that he would be heir of the world' (4:13; see Genesis 12:1–7). That word took centuries to take effect, but each step of fulfilment came about through faith.

1. Before Isaac was born, God showed Abraham the stars and said, 'So shall your offspring be' (4:18; see Genesis 15:5). Though Abraham and Sarah's bodies were 'as good as dead', Abraham believed that 'God had power to do what he had promised'. God gave life to Abraham and Sarah's bodies and enabled them to conceive a son (4:18–21). Thus, through faith, Abraham became the father of one and, as the generations passed, of an uncountable host.

2. Before Abraham's family themselves had become a nation, God said, 'I have made you a father of many nations' (4:17; see Genesis 17:5). Now, Paul says, when people from any nation believe, God declares them righteous. Since their faith and God's declaration follow God's pattern with Abraham, these people also are counted as members of Abraham's family (4:11–12, 16). If they got themselves circumcised, they would become Jews and lose their ethnic identity. Thus, it is through faith, not through the law, that believers from every nation become Abraham's offspring, and that Abraham has become the father of many nations.

Paul's and his friends' faith is in 'the God who gives life to the dead and calls into being things that were not'

(4:17). Since God proved this when he 'raised Jesus our Lord from the dead', they should not be surprised when God credits righteousness to the unrighteous, simply because of their faith (4:5, 23–25).

Thus ends part 1 of Paul's argument: God reveals his faithfulness and righteousness when he condemns sin. But, since he presented Jesus' blood as a sacrifice that covers sin, God also reveals his righteousness when he sets believers right. That is marvellously good news!

So, now that Paul's friends have believed and God has spoken and said that they are righteous, how should they live? What is the ongoing role of faith and righteousness? And how does all this connect to God's love for Jesus' people whom he calls to be holy?

The Son and the Spirit enable believers to live right, 5:1—8:39

God's gift of righteousness through faith – that flows from God's faithfulness and righteousness and was expressed in Jesus' faithfulness – continues as a life of faith and righteousness. As Paul wrote earlier, 'The righteous will live by faith' (1:17). God enables this life for Jesus' people, whom he loves and to whom he has given his Holy Spirit.

Through Jesus' death, the God who loves us has made peace with us, 5:1–11

Paul's pronouncement of God's good news continues. This short section pulls together many of the themes from the first big part of his letter (1:18—4:25), and it introduces several of the themes for the second part.

First, looking back, Paul and his friends have peace with God, because God has reconciled them to himself. So they need no longer fear wrath; when God judges each person, he will save them from his wrath (1:16, 18; 2:5, 8; 5:1, 9–11).

Second, these lines celebrate the magnificence of God's love and grace. God has declared Paul and his friends righteous because God presented Jesus' blood as a sacrifice that covers sins (3:24–26). And God did this – that is, Christ sacrificed his own life – when they were still impious and sinful (5:6–8). This is love beyond compare!

God demonstrates his own love for us in this: while we were still sinners, Christ died for us.
ROMANS 5:8

Looking back, Paul sees wrath that no longer threatens. Looking around, he sees righteousness and peace – both the fruit of grace in which they now stand. (Paul will develop this theme in 5:12—6:23.) And looking further forward, he sees God's glory, the glory all humans had failed to live up to (3:23). (Paul will develop this theme in 7:1—8:39.)

But, as it normally does, glory follows struggle, for pain is the tool that changes our very being. The path to realising our role as God's glorious children produces character because it winds through sufferings and demands perseverance (5:3-4). Hope sustains this venture, and it will not disappoint us – we will not be ashamed along the way – because God has already given us his Holy Spirit and poured his love into our hearts (5:5). As Paul will repeat in 8:18-39, when we suffer, we should not think that God has stopped loving us. We should think instead that he is making us glorious.

God's grace – and Jesus' righteous act – are greater than sin and death, 5:12–21

And now to the argument in more detail: the spread of sin and death through one human person to all people is analogous to the spread of righteousness and life through one human person to all people (5:12, 18). Sin's spread is analogous, but so much smaller.

Yes, when one human person (whose Hebrew name *Adam* means 'human person') disobeyed, sin and death entered the world, and, since all humans sin, death has spread out to all of them (5:12). And, yes, when one human person obeyed, righteousness and life came along and are now a gift for all (5:18–19).

But, head to head, the gift of righteousness is so much more than sin and its deadly consequence, for the gift overcomes sin and death. Though they were sinful and condemned, when humans 'receive God's abundant provision of grace and of the gift of righteousness', they will live and reign with Jesus Christ (5:15–17)! God's grace and Jesus Christ's righteousness have enabled a new way of being human, restoring the essential qualities of God's righteousness, goodness, kindness and life to the human vocation of reigning as God's glorious image-bearers (5:17, 21).

Grace is greater than sin and death. Death reigns over humans, whether sin is uncounted or whether the law exposes its innumerable instances. But grace is always greater.

Just as sin reigned in death, so also grace might reign through righteousness to bring eternal life through Jesus Christ our Lord.
ROMANS 5:21

Baptised people share Jesus' experience of dying to sin and coming alive to God, 6:1–14

Paul's assertion about grace prompts the other person to re-enter the dialogue.

PAUL   Where sin exceeds, grace superabounds (5:20).

PERSON   So what? Should we carry on diligently in sin so that grace may superabound (6:1)?

PAUL   Never ever! How is that even possible? Something happened when we were baptised. Each of us was somehow brought into Christ's personal experience:

through that ritual, we were buried with him. But that joining up with Christ begins before his burial and it extends beyond it (6:2–3).

Believers' union with Christ's personal experience begins with his death. Sin had corrupted their body's desires, occupied their body and enslaved their parts. However, when Christ was crucified, their 'old person' was crucified with him. This gruesome symbol is actually a glorious reality. Runaway slaves can be recaptured, but dead people cannot be owned. Since their old person is now dead, believers have been set free from sin's domination once and for all (6:3–7, 12–14).

The believers' union with Christ's personal experience continues with his life. Just as they died and were buried with Christ, so also they will be raised and live with Christ (6:5, 8–10).

We were therefore buried with him through baptism into death in order that, just as Christ was raised from the dead through the glory of the Father, we too may live a new life.

ROMANS 6:4

The front line between sin and grace, life and death, runs through the human body, the same body that was baptised. So, though they still live in a mortal body, Paul instructs believers (1) to regard their old self, which sin ruled, as dead, (2) to regard themselves as brought to life and (3) to offer all their parts to God as tools for doing right things (6:11-13).

This is what it looks like to live under grace, not the law (6:14).

So believers should present their bodies to God to do right and become holy, 6:15-23

PAUL   You are not under Moses' law, but under grace (6:14).

PERSON   So what? Should we sin, since we're not under the law, but under grace (6:15)?

PAUL   Never ever! If you carrying on sinning, you'll return to being sin's slave again, and the wages sin pays is death.

The choice is stark. Paul tells his friends they may be either sin's slaves or God's. Their former master compelled them to a sinful – and frankly shameful – existence culminating in death (6:16, 21–23). Their new master urges them to righteousness and holiness and offers eternal life in the end (6:16, 18, 22–23). Thankfully, they have obeyed – from the heart – this 'new pattern of teaching' (6:17).

But since they are subject to the same limitations as all humans, how are they to serve righteousness and pursue holiness? For sin had overrun their parts, and their body is still mortal and their flesh weak (3:13–18; 6:6, 12–19).

Just as you used to offer yourselves as slaves to impurity and to ever-increasing wickedness, so now offer yourselves as slaves to righteousness leading to holiness.
ROMANS 6:19

Since Jesus died, the believers are not bound by Moses' law; now the Spirit makes them alive, 7:1–6

Death ends obligations. It ended the enslavement of believers and their bodies to sin (6:6–7). It ends a woman's obligation to her deceased husband; now she may marry another man (7:2–3). And it ends everyone's obligation to the law; now they may give themselves to another (7:1, 4, 6).

Paul compresses into two sentences what he will unpack in 7:7—8:17. As sin had taken over the human body made of weak flesh, so too it appropriated Moses' law to accomplish its own ends. As Paul will illustrate in 7:7–8, the law said well, 'You shall not covet.' But sin used that law to activate 'the stimuli of sins' in Paul's and his friends' parts, exposing their senses to desirable things. The 'fruit' of those processes in their physical bodies was death (7:5).

But now, since Paul's brothers and sisters have died, the law is no longer the guiding force in their lives. Now they belong to Christ, and the Spirit directs and enables a new way of living and bearing fruit (7:4, 6).

Moses' law, although holy, could not cure sin's infection in my weak body, 7:7–25

PERSON   So is Moses' law sinful (7:7)?

PAUL   Never ever! Sin seized the law as an opportunity to trick me. Sin produced all sorts of sinful desires in me and

PERSON	killed me. No, 'the law is holy, and the commandment is holy, righteous and good' (7:8–12).
PERSON	So did the good commandment become the thing that killed me (7:13)?
PAUL	Never ever! It's the other way around. Sin used the good commandment to kill me. The good commandment showed how utterly sinful sin is (7:13).

Paul now launches into a detailed description of sin's assault on the human person, whom he here speaks of as 'I'.

Identifying the 'I'

Personally, the *I* is any one of Paul's friends who can identify with the *I*'s struggles. They experience a war within their own person. They want to act one way, but they end up doing quite the opposite, and their conscience often accuses them (7:15–25; see 2:15).

Biblically, the *I* is someone quite like the devout Israelite who composed Psalm 119. They believe and love God's word (Psalm 119:42–48, 163–167), but they still go astray (v. 176). They have not yet received the Spirit that God promised to give the Israelites in the new covenant. As God said, 'I will put my Spirit in you and move you to follow my decrees and be careful to keep my laws' (Ezekiel 36:27).

Diagnosing the *I*'s problem
The *I*'s problem is not with their deep, inner wanting. The *I* is someone who, from their very heart, wants to obey (see 6:17). Thus, this person is quite unlike the general human population, whose thoughts and motives are corrupted by sin (3:11–12).

Rather, the *I*'s problem is that they are 'fleshy' (7:14). (The NIV translates this as 'unspiritual'.) Their problem is that they have a mortal body, made of weak flesh, that is still commandeered by sin (7:14, 17–20, 23–25; see 6:6, 19; 7:5).

The *I* distinguishes between two aspects of their person:

1 **The *I*'s flesh is the physical substance of their body and its parts.** Good doesn't dwell there, but sin occupies it (7:17–18, 20, 23–25). (Thus the NIV often translates flesh as 'sinful nature'.)
2 **The *I*'s own self (their *ego* in Greek) is their inner person or their mind (7:22–25).**

The war within the *I*'s own person is between these two aspects. Sin occupies the flesh. Sin subverts the body's desires (see 6:6). Sin appropriates the good law that the *I*'s mind loves and uses it to assault the *I*'s parts with experiences that tempt them to sin (7:22–23; see 7:5). Through the *I*'s flesh, they are enslaved to sin, doing again and again what their evil captor causes them to do (7:14, 17, 19–20, 23). Yet the *I* is still responsible for the things they do, and they are miserable:

What a wretched man I am! Who will rescue me from this body that is subject to death?
ROMANS 7:24

But the Spirit enables Jesus' people to live right as God's children, 8:1–17

God's Spirit gives life to the people who are in Christ Jesus. And the way the Spirit uses the law sets them free from the way sin appropriated the law and used it to enslave them to sin and lead them to death (8:2). So now there is no condemnation for the people who are in Christ Jesus (8:1).

Here's how all this works out.

1. **God condemned sin (8:3).** God did this by sending his own Son to take on flesh like the flesh that sin occupied and then presenting his Son's body, made of flesh, as a sacrifice that covers sin (see 3:24–26). Thus God condemned, not a human person, but sin itself in its assault on the human person.

2. **The Spirit helps Christ's people live (8:4).**
   a. The Spirit redirects their thinking. Formerly they thought about the flesh's matters; they were hostile toward God and unable to please him. Now they think about the Spirit's concerns: life and peace (8:5–8). But, of course, the I's problem was not with their thinking, but with their doing.
   b. The Spirit revives their bodies. Formerly, their bodies kept doing sin, whether they wanted to (see 1:24–32; 3:10–18) or not (see 7:14–25). Now, the Spirit who lives within them is the same Spirit who raised Jesus from the dead. He gives life to their mortal bodies now, enabling them to live right (8:10–11; see 6:4–6, 11–23). This is how the I is healed.

And if the Spirit of him who raised Jesus from the dead is living in you, he who raised Christ from the dead will

also give life to your mortal bodies because of his Spirit who lives in you.
ROMANS 8:11

3 **As Christ's people live with the Spirit's help, the law's righteous requirement gets fulfilled (8:4).** The Spirit directs and enables them to love with God's love (5:5–8). In this way, the law's essential requirement – that each person love their neighbour – is fulfilled (13:8–10).

These people whom God's Spirit leads are God's adopted sons, his children. The Spirit keeps telling them, 'You are God's child', and he teaches them to call God by the Hebrew word *Abba*, Father. They are also, along with Christ, God's glorious heirs – if they suffer along with Christ (8:14–17).

God always loves his children – however grim their circumstances – and he will make them glorious, 8:18–39

Living out the role of God's human children in this world involves difficulty. That was Christ's own experience (8:17–18).

When the first humans fell short of being God's glorious images and blessing the creation that was entrusted to their rule, God subjected creation to frustration (see Genesis 3:17–19). In the future new creation, God will raise his children from the dead and give them glorious new bodies like his Son's. Together they will reign over creation, and their reign will set creation free from its frustration. Till then, creation waits and groans (8:19–22, 29–30).

So too do God's children. First, their bodies are not yet redeemed, and they continue to suffer the difficult experiences described in 7:5—8:13 (8:23–25). Second, they don't know what to pray for as God's representatives (8:26). And, third, trouble, hardship, persecution, famine, nakedness, danger and sword loom threateningly (8:35–36).

When difficulty disheartens God's children, Paul's words are clear:

1 **The Spirit helps you (8:23–27).** He intercedes for you.
2 **God is not against you; he is for you (8:28–32).** God knew you before you knew him. He loved you when you hated him.
3 **God uses all your experiences to make you like**

his glorious Son (8:28–32). That is the destiny he has determined for you.
4. **God does not condemn you; he declares you righteous (8:33–34).**
5. **Nothing at all can ever separate you from God's love in Christ Jesus (8:35–39).**

For I am convinced that neither death nor life, neither angels nor demons, neither the present nor the future, nor any powers, neither height nor depth, nor anything else in all creation, will be able to separate us from the love of God that is in Christ Jesus our Lord.
ROMANS 8:38–39

6. **Whether the trouble is mundane or extreme, you are super-conquerors (8:37).**

God has been and will be faithful to Israel, 9:1—11:36

Promises like these are inspiring… unless, of course, they follow a long string of broken promises; then they're just plain insulting. If the God who swears such love has in fact neglected his promise to Abraham and rejected his people Israel, then what comfort in life are his protestations, and what hope in death?

God's word to Israel didn't fail; God's people are those he chooses to have mercy on, 9:1–29

It is not as though God's word had failed. For not all who are descended from Israel are Israel.
ROMANS 9:6

When the first premise in Paul's argument contains a simple contradiction, we know we will need to read the whole argument intelligently and patiently till we understand what he's actually trying to say.

By way of introduction, Paul shares his heart and God's. Paul would offer himself for his own people. And God, who gave Israel many advantages, has himself offered his own life, in his Son Jesus the Messiah, for his people (9:1–5; see 3:1–2, 25–26).

Next, Paul argues for the principle that God the creator is free to do what he chooses (9:6–21).

God has mercy on whom he wants to have mercy, and he hardens whom he wants to harden.
ROMANS 9:18

In Genesis, that principle applied when God chose to extend the promise of adoption as his children to

Isaac, but not to Abraham's other sons, and to Jacob, but not to Esau (9:7–13). The effective factor, then, is not 'human desire or effort', but God's mercy (9:16).

Paul acknowledges that some of his friends will find this principle difficult. But he doesn't compromise the principle; instead, he corrects their perspective. To paraphrase: 'You've never questioned whether potters have the right to form a container from earth for whatever purpose they want. Why do you doubt whether God has the same right with the human persons he forms from earth?' (9:20–21).

Then Paul goes on to present God's relationship with Israel as a story of exceptional mercy, not baseless injustice (9:22–29). God is very patient with the 'wrath containers', hard-hearted people who have been storing up wrath against themselves for the day of God's wrath (9:22; see 2:4–5). He is patient with them in order to show his great glory to the 'mercy containers' (9:23).

So, for example, through the prophet Hosea God told Israel, 'You are not my people.' But then, after rebuking them severely, he promised that they would be called 'children of the living God' (9:26, quoting Hosea 1:10). Paul even finds in God's words a suggestion that God will also call non-Jews 'my people' (9:24–25, quoting Hosea 2:23).

Many within Israel didn't know that God's righteousness comes from faith, not from actions, 9:30—10:21

PERSON [*bewildered*] So… the other nations, who weren't 'chasing' righteousness, have got righteousness (through faith). But Israel, which was chasing Moses' 'law as the way of righteousness', never caught up to the law? How's that? (9:30–32)

PAUL Because they tried to accomplish it with their actions without relying on God. They tripped over the thing they should have trusted. (9:32–33)

The problem, as Paul the Jew explains it, is that many Israelites didn't know that righteousness comes from God through faith, so they tried to establish their own righteousness by keeping the law (10:2–3). And, as Paul will say in the following chapter, because many Israelites did not believe, they disobeyed God (11:11–12, 20).

Further, on Paul's reading, Moses himself taught that righteousness is from faith (10:5–8). After Moses repeated the law to Israel, he insisted, 'What I am commanding you today is not too difficult for you… No, the word is very near you; it is in your mouth and in your heart' (Deuteronomy 30:11, 14). 'That word that Moses mentioned is the faith that we've been talking about', Paul explains (10:8).

And, as both Isaiah and Joel said, faith and salvation are open to people from any nation, since the Lord Jesus is 'Lord of all' (10:9–13).

The problem, then, is not with God or his message. Moses and even the stars spoke, and Israel heard and understood (10:18–19, quoting Deuteronomy 32:21; Psalm 19:4). Rather, the problem is that some Israelites would not listen and believe (10:16).

All day long I have held out my hands to a disobedient and obstinate people.
ROMANS 10:21, quoting ISAIAH 65:2

God has mercy on disobedient people: some from Israel and the nations now, all Israel eventually, 11:1–36

PERSON   So, after holding out his hands all day long, did God eventually reject his people? (11:1)

PAUL   Never ever! For one, God has not rejected me. (11:1)

God did not reject his people, whom he foreknew.
ROMANS 11:2

In the days of Elijah, when Israel abandoned the Lord, God graciously chose to keep back some of them. 'So too, at the present time,' Paul says, 'there is a remnant chosen by grace' (11:5).

God's choice is driven by his grace, not by someone's actions. Though Israel is seeking righteousness, many of them have not obtained it. Instead, God has made them hard like stone: their spirit, eyes and ears do not perceive (11:7–10).

PERSON   Israel has 'stumbled', but have they 'fallen'? (11:11)

PAUL   Never ever! You must see the bigger picture:

1 **Israel stumbles and transgresses (11:11).** Part of them have become hard like stone (11:25), but a remnant has been chosen according to God's grace (11:2, 5, 7).
2 **Salvation and its riches go out to the other nations of the world (11:11–12).** The 'full number' of people from the other nations will come in (11:25).
3 **This inclusion of people from other nations will arouse Israel's zeal (11:11–14).** The whole of Israel will be accepted, and, in this way, 'all Israel will be saved' (11:12, 15, 25–26). God the deliverer will come from Zion and take away Israel's sins (11:26–27, quoting Isaiah and Jeremiah).

NON-JEW   Indeed! Branches were broken off so that I could be 'grafted in' to the 'olive tree' of God's people! (11:17–19)

PAUL   Granted, but not because you are somehow superior. It all depends on faith. A branch is connected to the root only through faith. God grafts in anyone who believes: non-Jews and,

> even more readily, Jews. So continue in God's kindness by continuing to believe (11:17–24; see 5:2).

Hardening may be partial, rejection may be for a time, but 'God's gifts and his call are irrevocable' (11:7, 11–15, 25, 29; see 9:25–26). Since everyone has disobeyed, everyone can receive mercy (11:30–32). Paul has made similar points already: grace overcomes sin (5:20); Christ died for sinners (5:8); God justifies the ungodly (4:5); everyone who calls on the Lord's name will be saved (10:13).

This third part of the letter that began as a defence of God's faithful love ends now in stunned wonder at the Lord's magnificence. No one can know the Lord's mind, and he owes no one anything (11:33–35).

For from him and through him and for him are all things. To him be the glory forever! Amen.
ROMANS 11:36

Paul calls believers to holiness and love, 12:1—15:13

Paul has presented (and defended) God's good news about Jesus. He has demonstrated that:

- the faithful and righteous God condemns sin but sets believers right (1:18—4:25)
- the Son and the Spirit enable believers to live right (5:1—8:39)
- God has been and will be faithful to Israel, 9:1—11:36.

At every turn, Paul has shown God's astonishing grace and his eternal love for Jesus' people. And now God calls the children he loves to be holy (see 1:7).

Since God has been so compassionate, offer him your bodies and let him renew your mind, 12:1–2

Therefore, I urge you, brothers and sisters, in view of God's mercy, to offer your bodies as a living sacrifice, holy and pleasing to God – this is your true and proper worship. Do not conform to the pattern of this world, but be transformed by the renewing of your mind. Then you

will be able to test and approve what God's will is – his good, pleasing and perfect will.
ROMANS 12:1–2

When God acts faithfully in righteousness, Paul calls it 'mercy'. And the only true and proper response to such compassion is whole-personed worship: reason offers the body as a sacrifice. As before, when the Spirit gives life to the believer's mortal body, faithful righteousness shows itself in the body's actions (6:4–23; 8:10–13).

This sacrifice is not for sins. God presented Jesus as a sacrifice that covers sins (3:25–26; 8:3; see Leviticus 1; 4—6; 16). Rather, this is the sort of sacrifice that celebrates the peace and fellowship that God's children enjoy with him now that he has saved them (Leviticus 3). As in the tabernacle, this sort of sacrifice is holy and pleases God, but, now, this sacrifice is one that remains alive.

Paul's friends will be transformed into this new way of living as the Spirit makes their minds new (see 7:6). Then, as they think about the Spirit's concerns, they will be able to test whether something is good, pleasing and perfect, and thus show that it is (or isn't) God's will (12:2; see 8:5–8).

By renewing their minds and giving life to their weak bodies, the Spirit enables God's faithful children to live a life that is demonstrably good, the good the I wanted to do before (2:7–10; 7:12–19). As they walk along with the Spirit, the law's righteous requirement gets fulfilled, and they will be more and more conformed to God's Son (8:4, 28). This too is nothing but God's grace.

By faith, build a good, loving and peaceable community, 12:3–21

As Paul thinks about his friends in Rome living a transformed life, he sees that the primary expressions of their sacred worship will be in their community, another 'body' that must be made holy.

So there is no longer room for some people to think that they are superior to others. We're all one body, we all belong to each other and each part has a different function. God has given some the grace to prophesy, to pass on a special message from God that builds his people up. He has given others special gifts to serve, teach, encourage, share, lead or show compassion. Do your part's special bit, Paul says, the thing God has made you good at (12:3–8).

Love must be the governing attitude. It flows, as always, from being loved, from experiencing love beyond description (5:5–8), from hearing the Spirit's insistent 'Your Father loves you, child' deep in one's spirit (8:15–16). And it expresses itself in a host of other good attitudes and actions, each of which builds a humble, other-oriented community (12:9–21).

Love must be sincere. Hate what is evil; cling to what is good. Be devoted to one another in love.
ROMANS 12:9–10

Love is defiantly good. It hates evil (12:9). When it is treated badly, it keeps doing good and refuses to avenge itself (12:17–19). But love's gentle kindness is powerfully subversive; it heaps burning coals on the enemy's head (12:20, quoting Proverbs 25:21–22). Thus, as God's children, who can never be separated from his love for them in Christ Jesus, respond to threat with love, they conquer evil with good (12:21; see 8:35–39).

Comply with civil authorities, 13:1–7

Second, the holiness of God's loved children shows up in their public lives (12:17–18). They comply with civil authorities, and they do good (13:1, 3).

Paul's reason is simple: 'the authorities that exist have been established by God' (13:2). In Rome in AD57, these words are ridiculous. People could perhaps imagine God appointing the former emperor Claudius – though even he expelled Jews from Rome. But Nero? Paul rephrases:

The one in authority is God's servant for your good.
ROMANS 13:4

Heard within the context of God's good news that Jesus is king and Lord, this restatement is quite a different assertion (1:4–5). Civil authorities are God's servants, his public officials (13:4, 6). But Paul's brothers and sisters are God's children, heirs, along with King Jesus, of the cosmos (4:13; 8:14–30).

So, as God's children, Paul says, honour the public servants your Father has appointed, and pay them what they are due (13:5–7).

Love each other – that satisfies the whole point of Moses' law, 13:8-10

Let no debt remain outstanding, except the continuing debt to love one another, for whoever loves others has fulfilled the law.
ROMANS 13:8

The debt of mutual love is present every time Paul's friends encounter a neighbour. They should focus on satisfying that obligation.

But as they do, Moses' law is also satisfied. For if they love their neighbour, they will not harm them by doing against them anything the ten commandments prohibit: adultery, murder, theft or coveting (13:9). 'Therefore,' Paul concludes, 'love is the fulfilment of the law' (13:10).

Love is the essence of faithful righteousness.

- Love is what Jesus Christ demonstrated when he died for his people (5:8)
- Love is how God feels about his children (1:7; 9:25)
- Love is what he has poured into their hearts through his Holy Spirit (5:5)

- Love is the eternal bond from which they can never be separated (8:35–39)
- Love is the definitive attitude among God's children (8:28; 12:9, 19).

Love is the good that believers do as God's Spirit makes their bodies alive and guides their thoughts to God's good, pleasing and perfect will. The gracious gift of Spirit-enabled love is how the law's righteous requirement gets fulfilled in their lives (8:4).

Act the part of Jesus, and don't make plans for what your flesh wants, 13:11–14

Paul's instruction is not only positive. He also has strong words of admonition.

The last hours of night are still dark. God's children's bodies still have desires; they continue to endure experiences that sin uses to tempt their flesh (Romans 6—7).

Disputes were a former way of life, and they seem to have infected relationships between the Jewish and non-Jewish members of the body (1:29; 2:1—3:20; 11:13–24). These differences were especially sharp on matters of food and drink (14; 16:17–18). And, of course, sinful desires were ever-present, not least sexual desire (7; 13:9).

'Wake up!' Paul says. 'Stop dreaming about how to do what your flesh wants. Get dressed. And remember to put on Jesus' clothes and carry along his tools, for today, as every day, that is the role you play' (13:11–14).

Rather, clothe yourselves with the Lord Jesus Christ, and do not think about how to gratify the desires of the flesh.
ROMANS 13:14

A believer's dedication to holiness is seen in their body, the words they say and the actions they do.

Accept the Lord's people, whatever their habits, 14:1—15:6

A number of the believers in Rome are bothered about how others were using their bodies. A few questions will guide us through Paul's concerns.

Who's doing what?

Some people are eating only vegetables and neither eating meat nor drinking wine (14:2, 21). Some are eating only meat from 'clean' animals (14:14). Paul describes these people's faith as 'weak' (14:2).

Some people eat anything and drink wine (14:2, 21). Paul may consider these people 'strong' (15:1). (Curiously, in many cultures, people in the first category are usually thought of as 'strongly religious'. This is another indicator that Paul's view of faith is not at all like our view of religion.)

Some observe particular days as special; others treat every day the same (14:5).

Why are they doing that?

Any of three reasons may be driving the 'weak faith' practices.

1 **Some people are following Moses' law (2:17–20).** They don't eat meat from unclean animals (Leviticus 11; Deuteronomy 14), and they observe the sabbath and other days Moses' calendar set apart (Exodus 20:8–11; Leviticus 23). The Lord gave Israel these laws to distinguish Israel from other nations, to show that they were his holy people.

2 **Some people may be observing the first day of the week as the 'Lord's' day (14:6; see Revelation 1:10).**

3 **Some people may not be eating meat or drinking wine because they don't want to risk communing with another deity.** For millennia, humans have eaten with their gods. The Lord instructed Israel to bring a tenth of their annual harvest to his house and feast on meat and wine in his presence (Deuteronomy 14:22–27; see Leviticus 3; 23). People from other nations also ate and drank with their gods (Judges 16:23–25). This was the practice Naaman the Aramean refused to continue with any god but Yahweh (2 Kings 5:17). And this is likely the reason Daniel and his friends refused the royal food and wine and ate only vegetables (Daniel 1:8–16; see Daniel 5:1–4; 10:3).

Food offered to idols arose as a real concern when people from other nations began to follow Jesus (Acts 15:29). Paul addressed this matter at length a few years earlier in a letter to the gathering of believers in Corinth (1 Corinthians 8—10). Since people from other nations offer their sacrifices to deities – and not to God – to eat food offered to idols is to commune with those deities (1 Corinthians 10:19–21).

What concerns Paul?
Paul is not concerned about their 'religious' practices. He is 'fully persuaded in the Lord Jesus, that nothing is unclean in itself… All food is clean' (14:14, 20).

The members of God's household live and die and do – or don't do – everything in between for the Lord (14:7–8). The Lord is honoured when people observe a day to him. And he is honoured when his people eat and thank him or when they don't eat and thank him (14:6).

Rather, Paul is concerned that his brothers and sisters are treating each other with contempt and judging each other (14:3). It is absurd for members of the household to criticise a servant who is accountable to the master – in this case, God himself! And it is outrageous for them to despise someone whom Christ died to accept (14:3–4, 10, 15)!

God can manage his own people, Paul insists, and he will (14:3–4, 11–12). So let him (14:13)!

What should they do instead?
First, love your brothers and sisters (14:15). Stop quarrelling; bear with each other. Build up, don't tear down, God's house. If doing something you enjoy would distress your brother or sister, or cause them to stumble from faith into sin, love them more than your own pleasure (14:1, 19–21; 15:1–2; see 9:31–33).

Second, live for the Lord. Faith will lead you to righteousness.

Everything that does not come from faith is sin.
ROMANS 14:23

So heed the Holy Spirit as he guides you to know what is right. If you think something is unclean, then for you it is. But keep your conviction between God and yourself. Don't bad-mouth something your brother or sister believes is good (14:5–8, 14–18, 22).

For the kingdom of God is not a matter of eating and drinking, but of righteousness, peace and joy in the Holy Spirit.
ROMANS 14:17

This is the way that Christ's servants live as holy sacrifices, pleasing to God (14:8–9, 18).

The nations will praise Christ their Lord, just as God promised, 15:7–13

Throughout Paul's letter to his friends in Rome, he is constantly aware of tensions between Jews and non-Jews. They criticise or despise the other, as though they are competing with each other for membership in a select group of God's favoured people.

Paul has confronted their antagonistic, us-them outlook time and again. But now he turns them round to see their differences from just the opposite perspective.

It has long been God's plan to bring Jews and the other nations together into the peace and joy of his kingdom.

God promised Abraham that he would be 'a father of many nations' (4:17–18, quoting Genesis 17:5).

Jesus – a descendant of Abraham, Jesse and David – is the one anointed to be king of Israel and all the nations (15:8, 12, quoting Isaiah 11:10). Through Jesus' death, resurrection and reign, God shows mercy to the other nations and so confirms his promises to the patriarchs (15:9).

When the nations respond by glorifying God for his mercy, they are fulfilling the next part of God's plan (15:9). This is what the prophets called them to do long ago (15:10–11, quoting Deuteronomy 32:43; Psalm 117:1).

So, Paul says to the Jews in Rome, when people from other nations hope in Jesse's Root and acknowledge him as king, recognise that Jesus Christ is doing something good for you, because this broad inclusion is what he promised your ancestors all along .

Accept one another, then, just as Christ accepted you, in order to bring praise to God.
ROMANS 15:7

Paul plans an apostolic visit to Rome, 15:14–33

Paul has heralded God's good news about King Jesus – the faithfulness, righteousness and love of God, Christ and the Spirit. And he has set out how Jesus' people should live right: in love that is holy. Now, with the purpose of his letter complete, he gets to why he has written it just now: I am coming to visit you.

First, Paul affirms his brothers and sisters (15:14–15). His letter has been 'quite bold' at points, but he wants them to know that he thinks they are actually good, knowledgeable and 'competent to instruct one another'. He has written them boldly because King Jesus appointed him foreign minister (15:15–16).

Second, Paul describes what his role entails. In a realm where the king is God, Paul, as priest, helps God's multi-ethnic subjects present – and, indeed, become – an offering that the Spirit makes holy and acceptable (15:16; see 12:1).

Christ and the Spirit advance the whole process. They work through Paul – as he announces God's good news and does miracles – to bring people to believe and obey a king of whom they'd never heard (15:16–21). This kind of holy dedication to king and kingdom is seen in the believers in Achaia and Macedonia, who are sending with Paul a contribution for the poor among the saints in Jerusalem (15:25–28).

Third, Paul asks for his brothers' and sisters' help. God's kingdom is becoming on earth as it is in heaven. Paul and his friends are flesh-and-blood humans living in Rome in real time and real space. But, by the Spirit, their speech and actions engage another dimension. Thus, though physically distant, they can join Paul's struggle – effectively – by praying for him. And, when they are together, they can aid him with rest and provisions (15:23-24, 28-32).

Paul blesses his friends, 16:1-27

Paul has concluded the last three sections with blessings for his brothers and sisters. The God of 'endurance and encouragement', who gives you the scriptures and his own example, lead you onward with hope (15:3-6). The 'God of hope' fill you with his Spirit's 'joy and peace' so that your hope overflows like his grace (15:13). And 'the God of peace be with you all' (15:33). Now Paul greets his dear friends personally and concludes with a final blessing for God.

Paul greets and encourages his friends, 16:1-23

Two things stand out in Paul's personal greetings.

First, both men and women play significant roles in the assemblies of the Lord's people:

- Phoebe, who bears this remarkable letter, is a 'deacon' (or servant) in the 'assembly' in nearby Cenchreae, Paul's honoured representative and his benefactor (16:1–2).
- Priscilla, along with her husband Aquila, is Paul's co-worker and hosts an assembly in her home (16:3–5).
- Junia is an apostle, as is Andronicus (16:7). And
- Mary, Tryphena, Tryphosa and Persis, along with Urbanus, also distinguished themselves in serving the Lord and his people (16:6, 9, 12).

Second, in his final instruction, Paul warns his brothers and sisters to avoid people who 'cause divisions' and who trip up the faith of others and land them in sin. With their 'smooth talk', they come off as both educated and devoted, but they are still enslaved to their belly. Don't get mixed up with them (16:17–19).

The grace of our Lord Jesus be with you.
ROMANS 16:20

Paul praises God for bringing the nations to obedient faith, 16:25–27

Now to him who is able to establish you in accordance with my gospel, the message I proclaim about Jesus Christ, in keeping with the revelation of the mystery hidden for long ages past, but now revealed and made known through the prophetic writings by the command of the eternal God, so that all the Gentiles might come to the obedience that comes from faith – to the only wise God be glory forever through Jesus Christ! Amen.
ROMANS 16:25–27

In Paul's final sentence, the themes of his letter converge:

- **The gospel** – the good news he proclaims that Jesus the anointed, who died for us and rose again, is now king.
- **The scriptures' mystery revealed** – that God always planned to include people from every nation who trust him in Abraham's family that he declares righteous, as he now is.
- **Faith's obedience** – faithful faith has always been the only way to obey God and please him.

Although this is a letter to his friends, Paul's final words are not to them. Rather, as priest, he presents his letter itself to God as an offering. All things, including this extraordinary letter glowing with the magnificence and mercy of God, are for God. To him be glory forever through Jesus the anointed! Amen.

4

Romans among other New Testament writings

Paul's letter to his brothers and sisters in Rome has much in common with the other earliest Jewish-Christian writings. It is also strikingly different from them at points, in places almost contradictory.

Writing the next chapters in the same story

Written as they were by Jews who read and believed the Hebrew scriptures, most of the earliest Christian writings appear as recent chapters in the same story. They accept the Hebrew scriptures as the words the one creator God entrusted to his people. They appreciate God's special choice of Abraham and his descendants to be his people. They honour Moses' law as good and wise instruction for a holy life. And they expect God to gather his people again, purify them and anoint a Messiah as their king. In these general ways, they are roughly similar to most other early Jewish writings, including the documents now collected in the 'Apocrypha', the Dead Sea scrolls and the first-century scholars Philo and Josephus.

However, the writings collected in the New Testament are distinct from other early Jewish writings on two counts. First, all but one of them (3 John) present Jesus as the Messiah whom God anointed to shepherd his people as king. Second, most of them recognise that the prophetic trajectory set by Moses, David, Isaiah, Jeremiah, Ezekiel and other prophets was projected to include believers from the other nations together with Israel as the people God blesses.

This second point appeared mysteriously, and it perplexed Jesus' followers for quite some time. What does it mean to 'include' non-Jews with Jews in God's people? Who needs to adjust, and how? What now of the distinctive law God gave Israel through Moses?

These are key questions in Galatians, and they are some of the questions that give rise to differences between Paul's letters and other early Jewish-Christian writings like James, Matthew and Hebrews.

Romans and Galatians

Among his letters that we still have, Paul's letter to his brothers and sisters in Rome is most similar to the letter he wrote about nine years earlier, in AD 48, to the assemblies of Jesus' followers in Galatia.

Faith is a dominant theme in both letters. Righteousness comes from faith, as seen in God's response to Abraham's faith. Both letters address the problem of sin, especially its enslavement of the weak flesh (through its external stimuli and internal desires) and its subversion of Moses' law. Both letters present Jesus' death and the Spirit's life as God's gracious initiative to free humans from sin and enable them to live a life of righteousness, seen essentially in love for one's neighbour. And both letters insist that God promised to bless all nations through Abraham.

However, the inclusion of non-Jewish believers along with Jewish believers brought about a set of concerns in the assemblies in Anatolia (modern Turkey) in 48 that was different from those in the assemblies in Italy in 57.

In the Galatian assemblies, some 'agitators' (inspired perhaps by a group who came from James in

Jerusalem) were compelling non-Jewish believers to live like Jews. They should adopt Moses' law, especially the distinct practices of circumcision and the festivals.

Paul's letter opposes their teaching forcefully. First, if believers from other nations get circumcised, they will become Jews. And if they are all Jews, then God's promise to bless all nations through Abraham will fail.

Second, Paul insists that life, righteousness and the inheritance God promised Abraham never came from the law; they always came from faith. Freedom from sin's enslavement of the flesh comes not from practising distinct rituals that Moses prescribed; rather, it comes from dying with the Son and living by the Spirit.

In the Roman assemblies, the tension came from both directions. Both Jews and non-Jews were judging and despising each other. So, in defence of non-Jewish believers, Paul's letter makes many of the same points about the nations, the law and the life of faith (dying with the Son and living by the Spirit). But then, in defence of Jewish believers, it goes on to defend the special place that Israel had and still has with God. Finally, the brunt of Paul's apostolic boldness falls more on the divisive attitudes (and especially the divisive people) than on the issues over which they are divided.

Romans and James

Of the early Jewish–Christian writings collected in the New Testament, few are as unlike each other as Romans (or Galatians) and James.

James may well have been written in the 40s by Jesus' younger brother, the leader of the assembly in Jerusalem (see Matthew 13:55; Acts 15:13). Alternatively, it could have been written by another James sometime later. But, whether written before Galatians or after Romans, James sees one key issue very differently from them.

JAMES 'You see that a person is considered righteous [or justified] by what they do and not by faith alone' (James 2:24).

PAUL 'For we maintain that a person is justified by faith apart from the works of the law' (Romans 3:28; see Galatians 2:16).

This contradiction left the German scholar Martin Luther unimpressed with James' letter and uncertain of its worth. And many of Luther's Protestant offspring have stumbled into the same quandary.

But James and Paul have quite different concerns. James is rightly bothered about people who claim to have faith in the one God but whose behaviour suggests quite the opposite (2:14–19). So James asserts, 'faith without deeds is useless' (2:20).

And he proves his point from Abraham's life. When 'Abraham believed God… it was credited to him as righteousness' (2:23, quoting Genesis 15:6). But that 'scripture was fulfilled', and Abraham's 'faith was made complete', when Abraham did something, 'when he offered his son Isaac on the altar'. God justified Abraham – that is, he considered him righteous – 'for what he did' (2:21). Abraham's 'faith and his actions were working together' (2:22).

As Paul writes his brothers and sisters in Rome, he shares James's concern. People who call themselves Jews are boasting that they have received God's law through Moses. However, apart from a missing piece of skin, there is little evidence in their lives that they actually heed God's law (2:17–29).

Paul warns them sternly. 'It is not those who hear the law who are righteous in God's sight, but it is those who obey the law who will be declared righteous' (2:13).

Paul couldn't be much clearer. But his clarity at this point actually confuses his equal clarity at other points in his own letter. For example, a few lines later Paul writes, 'No one will be declared righteous in God's sight by the works of the law' (3:20), and then he says, 'A person is justified by faith apart from the works of the law' (3:28).

The perceived tension between Paul and James is just as strong between Paul and Paul.

This is because Paul is concerned at an even deeper level that many Jews who are keen to keep God's law are trying to do so in action alone, *without trusting God* (10:2–3). But for Paul, 'everything that does not come from faith is sin' (14:23).

Here, then, is the dilemma rephrased from that perspective.

JAMES   'Faith without deeds is dead' (James 2:26).

PAUL   Deeds without faith are sin (Romans 14:23).

The way out of the dilemma lies along the path of Abraham's life of faith.

Both Paul and James quote Genesis 15:6; 'Abraham believed God, and it was credited to him as righteousness' (Romans 4:3; James 2:23).

Both Paul and James show that Abraham's faith was faithful, that his faith showed itself in action. Paul tells how Abraham's faith in God's promises strengthened Abraham's body to conceive a son with Sarah (Romans 4:17–22, quoting Genesis 15:5; 17:5). James tells how Abraham's faith enabled him to offer 'his son Isaac on the altar' (James 2:21; see Genesis 22:1–12).

For Paul as for James, real faith is faithful; it acts. God's faithful children must do what he considers good and right, and he enables them to do so through their trust in him (Romans 6:13–19; James 2:14–26; 3:17–18; 5:16). And for both James and Paul, the essence of faith's righteous action is love (Romans 13:8–10; James 2:8).

Romans and Matthew's gospel

On some readings, Paul's letter to the Romans could seem out of touch with the Jesus of the gospels. The gospels present the life, teaching, miracles, death and resurrection of Jesus of Nazareth. Romans discusses the death and resurrection of Jesus Christ, the Son of God. But, looking again at Romans, many of the themes Paul develops connect not only with (Paul's interpretation of) Jesus' death and resurrection but also with Jesus' life as recounted in the gospels. We'll compare Romans with the gospel called 'Matthew's'.

1 **Jesus is the anointed king and the Son of God.** Both Matthew's gospel and Romans open with the claim that Jesus is the 'Messiah' or 'Christ' – the one anointed to be king – a descendant of David. In the gospel, Jesus is conceived through the Holy Spirit and named 'Immanuel', God with us. In Romans, Jesus is 'God over all' (9:5). The gospel shows Jesus the king delivering his people from sin and other oppression, healing them, providing for them and teaching them. Paul shows Jesus loving his people and giving his life for them as their king. In the gospel, Jesus, to whom all authority in heaven and earth has been given, sends his followers to instruct all the nations to obey Jesus

(Matthew 28:18–20). And in Romans, Paul is Jesus' messenger, calling people from every nation to the 'obedience that comes from faith'.

2 **Jesus taught and modelled love, a righteousness beyond the details of Moses' law.** In Matthew's gospel, simply doing – or not doing – the things the law prescribes is not enough. Jesus teaches a perfect righteousness like God's, that gives and forgives generously and is pure and true (Matthew 5:17–48). In Romans, such righteousness comes only from God through faith. In the gospel and in Romans, foods that people eat do not make them unclean. Rather, what is important is love for one's neighbour, which fulfils the law's righteous requirement.

3 **The events of Jesus' life fulfil the Hebrew scriptures.** Time and again Matthew's gospel notes that an event or an action fulfilled the law or an ancient prophecy (1:22; 3:15; 5:17; 12:15–21; 26:52–56, etc.). And, as we have seen, throughout Romans Paul connects his view of what it means to be Jesus' faithful people with the grand story of God, his people and his world narrated in the Hebrew scriptures. The faithful love and righteousness of Jesus and his people from every nation

are the outworking of God's faithful love and righteousness.

Romans and Hebrews

Finally, the letters we call Romans and Hebrews are also quite different from each other. Romans calls Jews and non-Jews to faithful love and righteousness by dying with the Son and living with the Spirit. Hebrews calls Jews to keep following Jesus faithfully and not go back to their former way of being God's people. Yet in both letters, Jesus' sacrifice is centrally important, and believers themselves continue to offer sacrifices.

Hebrews shows Jesus as the perfect high priest who offered himself as a sacrifice for sin and presented his own blood in the Lord's sanctuary in heaven. His blood cleanses his people from their sins. Romans shows God as the one who presents Jesus and his blood as a sacrifice for sin. Jesus' blood covers his people's sins.

Hebrews instructs its readers to continue to offer not a sacrifice for sins – for Jesus' was the final sacrifice for sins – but 'a sacrifice of praise – the fruit of lips that openly profess his name' (13:15). And, Hebrews says, 'God is pleased' with the sacrifices like doing good and sharing with others (13:16).

Similarly, Romans instructs its readers to offer their bodies as living sacrifices, holy to God. God is pleased when they love and honour each other, share with each other and overcome evil with good.

5

The continuing message of Romans

Romans is a letter for the ages. Paul's view of God and his understanding of the human person and behaviour reshape the way we see God and ourselves. Paul's theology of the Son, the Spirit and the life of faith instruct us. And even Paul's long response to quibbling over food habits challenges us with surprising relevance.

God's freedom, righteousness and love

Perhaps the section of Paul's letter to his friends that strikes us as the boldest is his defence of God's freedom. God makes human persons from earth, and he is as free to do with them what he chooses, as a potter is with a vessel he or she makes from clay. God, as God, has the right to have 'mercy on whom he wants to have mercy' and to harden 'whom he wants to harden' (9:14–21).

Paul's assertion of God's ethical freedom is staggering, but – once we manage to get over the affront to our sense of human dignity – so too is his assertion of God's ontological bigness. God is eternal and powerful. He made the cosmos. He is not susceptible to being obliged in any way. No one can even know his mind. No mere human has the perspective or the perception to assess God's motives and actions in context in any objective way. He is much too big, too old and too complex. He is God.

But God makes himself known. And, in Romans, the first thing we see about God is his righteousness, his faithfulness to his righteous character and his righteous covenants. God is and does right – always.

However, that too is disconcerting, for Paul asserts that God will judge every human person according to what they have done. And that too is an affront, in this case to our human urge for autonomy. Nonetheless for Paul, God's judgement of each one of us is as real and certain as Paul's plan to travel to Jerusalem.

Yet, in Romans, we see another thing about God: his love. And that love captures us. God knew us and loved us before we knew him. Indeed, while we were still in rebellion against him, Christ died for us. This is grace that loved us at our worst and faithfulness that will love us persistently forever.

Many of us have known about this love – or assumed it in principle – for years. And yet in seasons of difficulty or depression, we come to know it personally as though for the first time. If you have not before, sit and look yourself in the mirror and feel the Spirit's warm breath fill the depths of your inner being, as he says again and again, 'Your Father loves you, child.'

The human person and behaviour

Paul's view of the human person shapes the way we see ourselves, especially our motives and our actions.

The human person is both internal (the heart with its mind) and external (the body's many parts, made of flesh). The heart may desire, and so may the body. The fleshy composition of the body constantly senses stimuli, but it is weak.

Sin takes advantage of that weakness. It assaults the flesh with tempting stimuli, and it requisitions the body's desires.

Thus, you may find yourself loving God in your heart and desiring to do good, yet impeded by your body's weakness or even thwarted by its contrary desires.

Paul understands this conflict, and the directness of his words in Romans 7 evokes a fresh sense of empathy even across the centuries.

Sexual orientation

Some who read Paul's letter today – like some of his friends then – encounter this struggle in a particular form: sexual desire for someone of their own sex.

Paul's words in Romans 1:26–27 sound harsh. But three points are important to keep in mind as you hear them.

1 **Paul understands that some women and men experience real sexual desires that are different from the sexual desires that are 'natural' for most other women and men.** (Other influential writers in the ancient world, like Plato, understand this too.) And Paul appreciates that these desires, whether chosen or resisted, are real and consuming and that they compel people's actions.

2 **Paul does not distinguish homosexual activity as somehow more grievous than other sins.** In Paul's list, it follows idolatry and sexual sin generally and precedes evils as common as greed and gossiping.

3 **Throughout his letter, Paul insists that grace outruns and outreaches sin.** Disobedience actually qualifies you to receive mercy. And, for God's children, *nothing* can separate you from God's love for you in Christ Jesus.

The Spirit's life and leading

For believers in every age, few messages are as relevant as Paul's hope-inspiring words about God's Spirit. The Holy Spirit is the answer to the problem of being human, the struggle we have living with mortal bodies made of weak flesh and assaulted by sin. The Spirit makes our bodies alive. He redirects our thinking to what is good. He enables us to present our bodies and their actions to God as holy, living sacrifices that please him. As God's children, we live now with the constant experience of hope and peace as the Spirit transforms us to be and act more and more like God's Son.

Faith and love

Faith is the medium and love the mode of all righteousness. As God's righteous children live by faith, the Spirit will lead us to lives filled with his love. This love flows from the love that God has poured into our hearts through the Holy Spirit. And it flows out in love for our brothers and sisters, for our neighbours and our enemies. This love challenges a host of our bad attitudes, and its sincerity will be tested when others irritate us or do us wrong. But by walking this path with the Spirit and each other, we will come to know the 'joy and peace' that 'the God of hope' gives (15:13).

Faith and civil authorities

Faith hears what it cannot see. Around us we see political leaders who hold tremendous power. Some oppose God's children, in some places and times more than others. Others offer us a share of their power if we call them good and affirm their policies.

But faith hears the rumblings of a kingdom in another dimension, present yet mostly unseen. Faith has heard the good news that Jesus the anointed, God's Son, is king and lord and heir of the cosmos. And faith believes it. Faith like this challenges us to honour civil authorities whom we didn't chose and whose policies we reject, for faith has heard that they are our Father's public officials.

And faith like this rebukes the many times – past and present – when social power, especially in the form of nationalism, has seduced the church into its bed.

For faith is convinced that, in the realest way possible, it obeys a greater king. And faith follows that king in love that gives itself generously to empower the weak, to accept the different, to be reconciled with its enemies and to speak hope to people of every nation.

Faith and creation

Faith hears too that creation is groaning and waiting, all the more expectantly now that our eldest brother is the first to rise from the dead and has been named 'Son of God in Power'.

So by faith and by the Spirit's life-giving power, God's children seek now to fulfil the glorious task for which our Father first made us from the earth. Wherever we live on this earth, we extend the blessing of God's good rule to the land and creatures he has made. We nurture life and order and bounty. We serve and keep – each other and all creation.

For faith knows that our faithful service and suffering now conform us more to the likeness of God's Son, so that when our bodies are raised to new life as his was, we will be glorious like him. And our gracious reign will set creation free to flourish and rejoice.

Faith and Israel's future

Faith believes that God has been and will be faithful to his promises to Israel. God blessed the nation Israel with many advantages, but, apart from faith, those advantages produced no real benefit (3:2, 9; 9:4–5). However, Israel's time of partial hardening will come to an end, and all Israel will call on the Lord's name and be saved. In the end, along with his younger brothers and sisters from every nation, Jesus the Messiah – the offspring of Abraham and the heir of King David – will inherit not the land of Palestine, but the whole cosmos (4:13).

Nurturing diversity within the church

The section of Romans whose message seems least relevant to our lives may well be Paul's extended discussion of food habits. Jesus' Jewish apostles were so effective at making followers of all nations that many Christians do not know a Jew who follows Jesus. Most Christians have never felt pressure to follow Moses' law. And, in many countries, Christians have never pondered the issue of eating food offered to idols.

Yet Paul's words about food and festivals speak pertinently to our lives in at least two ways.

First, throughout his whole letter, Paul admonishes us to nurture diversity within the church. Paul believed God's promise to Abraham: 'I have made you a father of many nations' (4:17, quoting Genesis 17:5). And he interpreted it to mean that if Abraham were father to only one nation – the Jews – God's promise would not be fulfilled. Thus Paul insisted that the nations not accept circumcision, become Jews or adopt Moses' law. As God's children, non-Jews must maintain their cultural identities if they are to contribute their distinct ethnicities to Abraham's necessarily multi-ethnic family.

So too today, there is something about each individual's disobedience that emphasises the particular sort and extent of mercy that God extended his grace to show them. And there is something about each nation's distinct ways of being together and of serving the God they now worship that reflect God's glory in a unique way. These are differences to accept, not suppress. For then, when the whole host of Abraham's many-cultured children offer their many-hued bodies and their many-tongued voices to God in praise, that will be magnificence fit for eternity.

Accepting each other as God accepts us

Second, Paul's words about how our ancient Roman brothers and sisters regarded each other's food habits restrain our tendency to criticise or despise each other.

As God's Spirit leads God's children, he will prompt some new habits, allow some old ones and fill all of them with devotion and thanksgiving to our Lord. As faith matures, old ways will seem unnecessary, and new ones will strengthen us further. These are the gracious movements of God with his children, the Lord with his servants.

Yet how often we reprimand another one of our Lord's servants for doing something we do not understand! How often we despise another one of our Father's children for behaving in a way we no longer appreciate! And how easily smooth-tongued, divisive people seduce us with simplicity and moral certainty and turn us against our brothers and sisters, and thus against the Lord who died to accept them!

Divisive people are more numerous and more dangerous than divisive issues. Avoid them.

Attend instead to those whose sincere love, humble goodness and holy service show us our Lord and nurture our own faithful faith.

6

Questions for reflection and discussion

1. How have you understood the different titles Paul uses for Jesus (1:1–7)? Which one strikes you now as particularly meaningful? Why?

2. How do you feel about being both 'loved by God' and 'called to be holy' (1:7)?

3. When you hear the word 'righteous', what do you usually think of it? How does it feel? How is that different from or similar to what Paul means by 'righteous' (1:16–17)?

4. What do you make of Paul's statements about people who have sex with others of their own sex (1:26–27)? From what you know of Paul (from reading Romans or his other letters), how might a conversation between Paul and one of your gay friends go?

Questions for reflection and discussion

5 Have you thought before that God will judge everything you do (2:5–28)? How does that make you feel? What questions does it raise for you?

6 Are people as wholly bad as Paul makes them out to be? Do you think someone could do enough good on their own for God to call them righteous (3:9–20)?

7 Read through the ritual God prescribed for the Day of Atonement, or Yom Kippur (Leviticus 16). Compare that ritual with how Paul says God presented Jesus and his blood (Romans 3:25). What do you want to say to God about Jesus' death and God's free gift of righteousness?

8 Both Paul and James cite Abraham as an example of faith and righteousness (Romans 4; James 2). Do Paul's and James's approaches contradict each other? How might a conversation between them about faith have gone?

9 What words would you use to describe God's love for you (5:1–11)? Try writing them out as a prayer.

10 Which sin have you sometimes thought is too extreme for grace to reach beyond (5:12–21)?

If God's grace can reach even further than that, what is grace really like?

11 Which parts of your body do you struggle to use for righteousness? What would it look like to use each of those parts as a tool for righteousness (Romans 6)?

12 Have there been times in your life when you feel like the *I* in Romans 7? In what ways do Paul's words give you words to describe your experience?

13 How would you explain what it means to live 'according to the Spirit' or to have your mind 'set on what the Spirit desires' (8:1–13)? Do you know someone whose life looks like they are living that way? How do they explain it?

14 Sit in front of a mirror and look yourself in the face. Then let God's Spirit speak his own testimony all the way down into the bottom of your heart. Listen as he says again and again, 'Your Father loves you, child.' Keep listening until you can accept his words as real (8:14–17).

15 From Paul's brief description, what do you think life on earth might look like when God's children are revealed (8:18–23)? How does that vision influence the way you think about and live on earth now?

16 When one of your friends is going through a particularly hard time, how would you use Paul's words in Romans 8:18–32 to encourage them?

17 What do you think of Paul's argument about the potter's rights and God's rights (9:20–21)? Have you thought about that before? Is the argument sound? How does it make you feel?

18 How do you feel about the way God offers mercy, even toward those who won't listen (9:22—10:21)?

19 Explain the way Paul connects people's disobedience and God's mercy in 11:11–32.

20 Does Paul's metaphor of offering your body as a holy sacrifice make sense (12:1)? In what ways do you see God renewing your mind and transforming your life (12:2)?

21 What sort of gift has God given you to share with the other members of Christ's body (12:3–8)? Which gifts do your friends see in your life?

22 Of the different ways that sincere love expresses itself, which ones stand out to you (12:9–21)? Which one comes most naturally to you? Which one had you not thought of before? Which one seems the most challenging?

23 Explain Paul's view of who civil authorities are and for whom they work (13:1–7). In what ways does his vision influence the way you think about and respond to public officials?

24 What does Paul mean by 'love' (13:8–10)? Does love really fulfil Moses' law? How?

25 What would it look like if you woke up tomorrow morning and played the role of the Lord Jesus Christ (13:11–14)?

26 In your church or among your friends, over which issues do people criticise or despise each other (14:1—15:6)? What sort of people or behaviour do you find it hard not to criticise or despise?

27 If 'everything that does not come from faith is sin', how do you want to change the way you approach life (14:23)?

28 In your church or society, what are the social differences that a majority group tends to suppress, whether intentionally or not? With which people who are socially different from you could you associate yourself (15:7–13)?

29 In what ways can you encourage your brothers and sisters to accept and affirm each other (16:17–19)?

30 Reflect on Paul's closing blessing in 16:25–27. How does it help you pull together your thoughts and feelings now that you've studied through Romans? Compose your own prayer that blesses God for the key things you have come to appreciate.

Further reading

Online resources

BibleProject, 'Romans': **bibleproject.com/explore/romans**

'Romans' in *ESV Global Study Bible* (Crossway, 2012): **crossway.org/bibles/esv-global-study-bible-ebook**

Books

Gordon D. Fee and Douglas K. Stuart, 'Romans' in *How to Read the Bible Book by Book: A guided tour* (Zondervan, 2002).

Craig S. Keener, *Romans (New Covenant Commentary)* (Cascade, 2009).

Douglas J. Moo, *Romans (NIV Application Commentary)* (Zondervan, 2009).

Tom Wright, *Paul for Everyone: Romans: Parts One and Two* (SPCK, 2009).